KATHRYN MORTIMER has been married to David for 30 years and is mother of Harriet and Sally, both in their twenties. Born in Liverpool, she moved to the South West of England at the age of 18 where she has remained ever since. She has a degree in Mechanical Engineering from the University of Bath, and a long career in Information Technology.

Drifting towards retirement in a steady 9 to 5 job, life was routine and predictable. But on Christmas Day 2017 that changed. After conversations with her daughters about their own employment choices, she made the completely unexpected decision to write a book. This started her fascinating journey into the world of publishing, and the strange, exciting world of the Millennial Generation.

HARRIET was born in Bristol where she attended Colston's Collegiate, then graduated from Royal Holloway University with a degree in Psychology. She worked in fund raising before abandoning corporate life to set up her own business. She is widely travelled, and is now a self-employed badminton coach and artist.

SALLY was born in Bristol where she attended Colston's Collegiate before dropping out of school with mental illness. Five years on, she is slowly winning the battle against debilitating anxiety and depression. After various part time jobs in shops, a dog groomers and doggie day care, she is now hoping to launch a career as an artist and author. Sally loves dogs, elephants and Old School Runescape.

Kathryn, Harriet and Sally Mortimer

MOTHER OF MILLENNIALS

Published in 2018 by SilverWood Books

SilverWood Books Ltd
14 Small Street, Bristol, BS1 1DE, United Kingdom
www.silverwoodbooks.co.uk

ISBN 978-1-78132-815-6 (paperback)
ISBN 978-1-78132-816-3 (hardback)

British Library Cataloguing in Publication Data
A CIP catalogue record for this book is available from the British Library

Page design and typesetting by SilverWood Books
Printed on responsibly sourced paper

To Harriet and Sally,

I'd like to say Dad and I decided to have children as a result of the genetic imperative to reproduce and contribute to the survival of the human race. I'd like to, but it would be a lie. The truth is you were brought into this world to fulfil the purely selfish desire of 2 thirty-somethings who wanted to experience parenthood.

For all our inadequacies, please accept we did our best. Take comfort that you can shape your own futures as part of a generation which is kinder, more inclusive and has a greater understanding of the human condition than ever before. If this isn't enough, be patient. You'll get an opportunity to exact your revenge when the time comes to choose our nursing home(s).

Love you.

Always and forever.[1]

1 Subject to you showing compassion in the choice of where you send us when we're too feeble to care for ourselves.

A Word about QR Codes

Many (dare I say most?) readers of this book will be active users of the Internet. Whether for on-line banking, shopping, researching your next holiday location, entertainment, catching up on world events, or any of a myriad of other activities, it's hard to contemplate life without it (Hard, but not impossible; my own mother is one example of an Internet-free zone.)

Anyway, throughout this book I make plenty of references to Internet resources, some of which you might want to check out for yourselves. Not a problem if you're reading an e-book—just click on the link and you'll be transported straight there. But if you're holding a physical book in your hand, you probably don't want to be typing in *https://www.youtube.com/watch?v=x2RJN9a_jdM* to watch a little pug falling over while she sings a jaunty Irish ditty. Thanks to Sally, you won't have to. She came up with the great idea of using QR codes instead. You can scan these neat little black and white spotty things with your phone, and it will take you straight to the site. Well, you can once you've downloaded a QR Code Reader app to your phone.

I know most of you will find the instructions that follow a bit like teaching granny to suck eggs. Bear with me, I don't like making assumptions when it comes to technology.

Android: Go to Google Play, search for QR Code Reader—there are dozens to choose from, and most of them are free. Select

Install. **Apple iPhone**: Same as Android, but get app from App Store.

All done? Great. Give it a whirl with this one. Launch the app, place the frame displayed on the screen of your phone around the spotty thing below, and hold still. In no time at all, your phone should ask you if you'd like to browse motherofmillennials.co.uk.

Of course you don't. You've got a book to read!

Contents

Prologue

It was the afternoon of Christmas Day 2017. We had exchanged our presents, and I was at home with Sally, who had recently celebrated her 21st birthday, and Rupert the staffy/labrador we'd adopted from a local animal rescue centre. While I was relaxing with my glass of barely drinkable non-alcoholic wine, my husband David was slaving away in the kitchen preparing our vegan Christmas dinner.

Earlier that day we had Skyped Harriet, our 25-year-old daughter, who was part way through a three-month holiday in the southern hemisphere. She was spending a perfect Christmas with friends on the stunning Pacific island of Fiji. When we started the call she was awash with her usual effervescent enthusiasm and in high spirits, but before long she had dissolved into tears while imparting some unexpected news.

Nothing dramatic—she wasn't ill, or pregnant, or in prison. Neither was it anything so awful I'd have to abandon my Yuletide plans (such as they were), don my Super Mum outfit and go scampering around the house in search of my passport. Then take out a massive online bank loan, jump on the next flight to God knows where, before busting her loose and rescuing her from her desperate predicament. No, mercifully not that bad. Yet the news was so upsetting for Harriet that she could only get her words out in short, clipped phrases, punctuated by deep, heart wrenching sobs—each one of which pushed my stress levels up a notch higher. I had no inkling of what was causing her such desperate distress.

Not to be out done, Sally chipped in with her own revelation that made this Christmas Day memorable. Both items of news related to employment. Harriet's great distress resulted from her realisation that, in her own words, 'I can't bear the idea of spending the rest of my life stuck in an office'. (It seems such a simple sentence—it's hard to fathom why she took a full two minutes to spit it out.) Sally's news? Well, she had just introduced her exciting plan to earn money by live-streaming herself playing Runescape. (If you're from a generation who has absolutely no idea what this means, you will be enlightened later.)

Rewind a quarter of a century. I was sitting in the same room gulping from a large glass of red wine, surrounded by the detritus that accompanied my first exciting Christmas as a mother. Meanwhile the same husband was slaving away in the same kitchen preparing a full turkey roast. Twenty-five years ago we celebrated Christmas as two thirty-something parents with high hopes for the future. Now, as I was getting uncomfortably close to the Big 60 (but not as close as David), it struck me I was indulging in something that is unusual for me. I was feeling sorry for myself and thinking 'where did I go wrong?'

Ordinarily I am an optimistic, glass half-full person. I am acutely aware that compared to the vast majority of people who have ever walked this earth, my life has been trauma-free. I've lived through peaceful times in a country I care deeply about. I grew up in a loving, stable family. I've never had to deal with sudden, unexpected loss or critical illness of loved ones. Mostly my career has been enjoyable, and my efforts more than adequately rewarded with a good, steady income. Of greatest importance, my life has been blessed with two beautiful daughters.

Despite all this good fortune, here I was on Christmas Day feeling downhearted. I don't recall how long I remained in this morose state. Twenty seconds? Maybe an entire minute. But soon enough my optimistic gene kicked back in and I hatched an idea for a New Year's resolution. 'You know what, Sally', I said to my daughter—who was by now engrossed in her world of Runescape—'our lives have become weird. I'm going to write a book about us.' 'Er, OK. That sounds awesome', she replied supportively, while wielding a Toxic Blowpipe with the sole aim of ruthlessly annihilating a pair of gigantic gargoyles. 'So what are you going to call it?' she added, demonstrating her admirable ability to hold a coherent conversation while concentrating on a computer game. While my conscious brain was forming the response 'I haven't thought about that yet', my subconscious stepped in to announce 'Mother of Millennials.' Just in case there was any doubt, I added 'I'm the Mother, you and Harriet are the Millennials.' And so this book was conceived.

This is a story about motherhood. It looks back over a quarter of a century of family life during which our two cherished daughters set out on their expedition towards adulthood, following a path determined for them by their loving, protective—but hopelessly incompetent—parents. In the early stages they followed the set path to perfection, except when they made effortless detours that enhanced their life experiences. However, as they progressed, the route became arduous and unsatisfying. One daughter realised the path was taking her to an unappealing destination; while the other succumbed to devastating mental health problems that brought her journey to a premature standstill.

It is a story of two daughters. One so similar to me I have often questioned whether her father's DNA made any significant effort during the process of fertilisation. The other, so different to both her parents the sensible conclusion is there was a mix up in the maternity ward. It poses questions such as how it is possible for one daughter to attract hordes of perfect, long-term friends like iron filings to a magnet, while the other shares her mother's many and varied social inadequacies. One who feeds greedily on social interaction, the other (again like her mother) fluctuates randomly between tolerance and active avoidance.

Mostly it is a Mother's-eye-view of the passage taken by the two afore-mentioned daughters in search of their natural position in life, and in the army of the gainfully employed. It follows their exhausting climb to the suffocating peaks of Qualification Mountain; their regimented and time-devouring march across the demanding landscape of Extra-Curricular Forest; their miserable trudge through the murky waters of Parental Expectation River, while desperately fending off the grotesque Mental Health Monsters that glided below the surface, stealthily tracking their weakening prey. Then on in hopeful search of the glorious sunlit Opportunity Meadows, where perfectly tailored careers grow in abundance, swaying in a gentle breeze, calling out 'Here I am. Pick Me. Please Pick Me'.

I hope you, the reader, will find this book entertaining, interesting and even enlightening. It has provided me with immense enjoyment and satisfaction since the idea of writing it first surfaced. It was triggered by the realisation that neither of my expensively educated daughters was following the path that was supposed to guide them on their odyssey from squealing newborn to successful, responsible and independent adult.

The book has provided me with a valid reason for retrieving my long-forgotten memories. It has also been an excuse to talk—and I mean really talk—to my daughters about what life has been like from their perspective. My weekly phone calls with my own mother have become far more interesting. Beforehand, our discussions revolved around what she'd had for lunch, her trips to Sainsbury's, or the well-being of Jeremy the zombie gnome who had taken up residence in her garden one dark Halloween night. Now we talk about Charles Bonnet Syndrome, the work of world-renowned neurologist Dr Oliver Sacks, and the mysteries of the human brain. Committing myself to this book has also provided me with an inventive and pressing excuse for shirking my housework responsibilities.

Like every parent I want my offspring to have happy and successful lives. But success is both subjective and relative. When I embarked on the odyssey into motherhood, what did I consider as appropriate measures of success for my daughters? Well, they would achieve academic success by attaining good GCSEs and A-levels, then moving on to a traditional university where they would be awarded an honours degree in a subject considered useful in the job market. An upper second class would be marvellous, but a lower second wouldn't be disastrous. Regular selection for their school netball, tennis, rounders or hockey teams would be celebrated as sporting success. A successful career didn't require either daughter to become a high-flyer or industry leader, a brain surgeon, rocket scientist or Governor of the Bank of England. No. An office-based job working for a respectable company, with good career prospects and earning a reasonable salary, would be spot on. Successful life skills would be measured from general achievements such as the number of good friends, the confidence to seek out and seize new opportunities, and the ability to select a good, loving man for a husband. OK, so let's be honest, 'wealthy' was also high on that list of desirable attributes. By the time they hit their mid to late twenties, success would also include financial independence, and having an affordable mortgage and their own home. A home I hoped would be within a reasonable travelling time, so as their lives progressed they'd have no problem visiting their aging parents, eventually with a car-load of grandchildren for us to spoil rotten. Basically, I set my expectations no higher than I had achieved in my own life (except the wealthy husband which continues to elude me). So how are they faring against these targets?

Harriet exceeded all sporting expectations. Not only did she represent her school in all the traditional sports played by girls, she was also a member of successful rugby and cricket teams. She reached the top level of junior county badminton, and even represented England at rounders. Academically she achieved everything I had hoped for, including an excellent upper second class honours degree in Psychology. She is well-travelled, incredibly sociable and—until recently—she seemed keen to build on her 3 years of experience in fund raising, which included a year at no less an institution than the University of Cambridge. But now, to use the terminology of the Millennial generation, she is an *emerging adult* who is going through a *quarter life crisis*. The intended outcome of this unexpected phase in her development is to divert her onto a path of her own choosing, rather than the one crafted for her by her parents. This is not an unreasonable goal, and I am more than happy to support her.

Sally also exceeded sporting expectations, although not so much in traditional school sports, all of which—except for rounders—she loathed. She did however excel in archery and, like Harriet, became a good county-level badminton player. She achieved a truly amazing set of top grade GCSEs before mental health problems forced her to drop out of school at the end of her first year in 6th form. Since then she has been engaged in an exhausting and often debilitating battle against anxiety and depression, watching helplessly from the side lines as her former school friends completed A-levels before disappearing off to university.

I have no interest in asking what 'went wrong' or what I could/should have done differently. Would their lives be different now—either better or worse—if I had not discovered David Lloyd Tennis Centre and got caught up in the ultra-competitive tennis scene? How would their lives have turned out if we had been unable to afford private education? Questions such as these serve no useful purpose as their answers are unknowable.

But what if I had been familiar with the term '*empath*', and believed the condition to be real? Could Sally's mental health problems have been *prevented* before they derailed her young life? Well, I'm now in no doubt the answer to this question is unequivocally 'Yes, they could'. But I didn't know, and I refuse to beat myself up about that. However, now I do know—and I have no doubt it is a real condition—it would be unforgivable of me if I failed to highlight it.

I worked very closely with Sally on the chapter *An Empath in the Family*. Our goal is nothing more ambitious than to raise awareness of the condition, and to point readers to professional resources for more information. This is not a self-help book, and we are not qualified to give advice. However, if you are a parent, teacher, coach, nursery worker, older brother or sister, or any other form of child carer, please dedicate a few minutes of your time right now to answering the following questions: Are any of the children in my care overly sensitive? Do they burst into tears or run and hide at the slightest admonishment or unkind word? Do they startle easily and take a long time to recover if, for example, a balloon bursts nearby? If any of these are true, it's possible the child is an empath. Please put aside any scepticism you have and don't ignore it or assume the child just needs 'toughening up'. With early intervention and the right development, being an empath could be the most wonderful gift, instead of the curse that has accompanied Sally throughout her life.

Enough of the serious stuff. What's done is done. My interest now lies in supporting both daughters as they map out futures that build on their strengths. Futures that align with their hopes and dreams, in a world full of opportunities that bear no resemblance to those available when I was their age. I'm now aware that I occupy a world in which Millennials are expertly taking over the reins from Baby Boomers and Generation X. A world Millennials are steadily turning into a better, kinder, more inclusive place.

While writing this book I have immersed myself in an ever-expanding cosmos of online material. Some hilarious, some enlightening, some deeply disturbing. I love the Information Age. Everything I could possibly want or need to know, available instantly from the comfort of my own home. 24 hours a day, 7 days a week. Bank holidays included. No more pesky, time consuming trips to libraries to research basic facts while I sit in silence. Need to confirm the author of *The Day of the Triffids* or check when the Sahara turned from fertile land to desert? Google it. Job done. Want to understand how the brains of procrastinators work? Just head to TED Talks on YouTube for everything you need to know. Don't know how many issues of Man, Myth & Magic were published in the 1970s? Well, I could phone Mum and ask her to count them, alternatively I could turn to Wikipedia for an instant—and probably more accurate—answer.

I should make it clear from the start that I make no pretence at scientific rigour behind any of my observations or conclusions. The contents of this book revolve around the actual real-life experiences of an unscientific sample that can be counted on the fingers of one hand; namely 1 Baby Boomer, 1 Generation X, 2 Millennials and a five-year-old dog. OK, so it's a little unfair to separate myself (Generation X) and my husband (Baby Boomer) into different categories, as only 3 years separated our births and we share similar hopes, expectations and values. But I'll do it anyway as our births straddle 1960, the year at which convention places an imaginary boundary. It has nothing to do with the fact it makes me feel so much younger than him.

My dear old mum pops up from time to time, and in truth she has a larger part than the dog. Still going strong well into her 80s, she is a member of the greatly respected Silent Generation who endured the horrors of World War II, and endowed generations that followed with stoicism and strong work ethics. What makes Mum so interesting in the context of this book is that I have recently discovered she has lived the last few years with a deep, dark secret. A secret so potent that she jealously guarded it for fear that exposure would result in her being carted off to the place described in a 1960s song by Napoleon XIV as 'the happy home with trees and flowers and chirping birds, and basket weavers who sit and smile and twiddle their thumbs and toes.' Honestly, this sounds a far more appealing prospect than the horrors she suffered bringing up 3 constantly warring children. But more about Mum later.

Before I get into the Mother part of the title, I will whizz through the first 25 years of my life. This is important because it explains the context in which I formed my own expectations for my daughters. A context in which the equation was simple—hard work is directly proportional to success. A context in which boy married girl, and the happy couple had kids and stayed together for life—even if somewhere along the way they became unhappy and fell out of love. A context in which the term 'mental health issues' hadn't been invented—or if it had, it hadn't hit mainstream awareness.

I now realise that life wasn't so black and white back then. It's just that as a Catholic, educated in a Convent Grammar School, and from a stable, hard-working family, I lived a sheltered life protected from bad things. Also, looking back over my first quarter of a century on this earth has highlighted just how ill-prepared I was for the responsibilities of motherhood. That both my daughters made it into their twenties at all is an amazing achievement on their part.

Then, we'll move on to the Millennials. I have handed over a chapter for Harriet and Sally to introduce themselves as they see fit. They have free rein to write whatever they want, and I'll admit to being a little nervous about what this will uncover. What new disturbing secrets will emerge? Will I get a single-page drawing of a black cloud spewing heavy rain drops onto a desolate, hunched figure with the words 'Life is Shit' scrawled across the page? Has their expensive education taught them the proper use of the apostrophe? Only time will tell.

The rest of the book skims the surface of the development of important themes; global warming and the environment, sexual orientations and freedoms, veganism and—a subject that is now close to my heart—mental health. It starts with how I viewed these movements in their early years when, through the eyes of a full-on introverted geek, they all appeared to be championed by small bands of oddballs. Most appeared harmless tree-hugging, forest-dwelling weirdos, while others were violent anarchists who threatened lives and livelihoods of good, law-abiding citizens. Citizens whose only crime was to be caught up in a line of business targeted by these unpleasant, crazed activists. From there I'll launch myself across the great expanse of time to today, where these causes have reached mainstream maturity and capture the zeitgeist of the Millennial generation. I do not attempt to throw any light on how we got from

A to B—that's a level of detail I'm happy to leave for those with time and energy to spare.

Finally, I'll talk about the start of my own Millennial-inspired *'three-quarter life crisis'*. I plan to emerge from my cocoon reinvigorated and eager to engage in what I hope will be a long, active and fascinating exploration through the uncharted waters of semi-retirement. Then, when I'm good and ready, I'll take my final breath and shuffle off this mortal coil, liberating my atoms for reuse in a timeless universe. If I could choose the future of my atoms, I'd want them to drift freely until they reintegrate for eternity in the form of a female duck-billed platypus, somewhere in the warm waters of the southern hemisphere. Freed from the constraints of a human body, I would have another opportunity to improve my skills as a mother without ever having to endure the pain and misery of pregnancy, child birth and breastfeeding ever again.

1

Growing up a Geek

To say I have always been a bit of a geek doesn't do me justice. A fuller description would include adjectives such as *painfully shy*, *studious* and, most prominent of my rich and varied inadequacies, *socially inept*. On the positive side, I was blessed with an endless supply of optimism and the genetic makeup that made studying almost enjoyable, certainly far preferable to socialising. There were many activities in which I excelled. Some, including my exceptional ability in all things mathematical, proved extremely useful and set me up for a rich and fulfilling career. Others, notably the ability of my 6-year-old self to accurately describe the offside rule to any adult who succeeded in engaging me in conversation, went a long way towards reinforcing the sense of weirdness that has been my cherished lifelong companion.

I credit a large chunk of my quirkiness to an inventive maternal fib, along with my misinterpretation of a simple English noun. These resulted in me growing up in the firm belief I was the daughter of a mad scientist father who would one day save the world from marauding plants. That, and a Transylvanian Gypsy mother who shared a bloodline with Dracula the Prince of Darkness himself. It was not fantasy—but rather painful real-life experience—that cast my older brother in the role of evil psychopath, while my younger sister was so normal and inoffensive that I barely remember her existence until I reached my late teens. (Sorry Sis).

My time at primary school would be unmemorable but for the excitement generated by Cilla Black's wedding in the church located just a stone's throw from the school. I was 7 years old at the time. My classroom was situated right next to the fire escape that led directly into the church grounds. On the afternoon of the wedding, the entire population of the school crammed into the room in the hope of catching a glimpse of Cilla. The teachers took turns to disappear through the fire escape, but the cold January weather ensured they did not stay outside for long. As soon as they returned, they would be replaced by another eager group. I managed to catch sight of the bride by sneaking out with the Deputy Head (my status of Teacher's Pet undoubtedly helped). It was only a glimpse, but it was enough to see something that caused me considerable confusion. Cilla appeared to be wearing the Leeds United football kit: white shirt, white shorts, long white football socks up to her knees, and white football boots. The thing I found strange about her attire was not that I thought she was wearing a football kit—but that it was Leeds United's. I knew for a fact Cilla was from Liverpool—her accent was a bit of a giveaway on that score. So why the white of Leeds United and not the blue of Everton or the red of Liverpool?[2]

Another lasting memory from primary school was that I was one of only two girls permitted to play football with the boys. This was a really big deal for me. It went a long way towards compensating for the excruciating daily pain suffered in my last year when the bell rang to signal home time. Rather than allowing us to leave, the Headmaster insisted on adding 30 minutes to our day, five days a week. For reasons unknown, he decided it was his duty to enhance the life skills of his young charges by reading to us from his endless supply of historical novels written by Jean Plaidy. A quick scan of Google confirms she wrote at least 78 of the damn things. Why would anyone think that was an acceptable way to treat ten- and eleven-year-olds, none of whom had been accused of anything more

2 Through the magic of Google, I have now established the cause of my childhood confusion—Cilla was wearing an *exceptionally* short white dress and white knee-length boots

terrible than a misspelt word or two? I have vivid memories of getting through the repeated ordeals by sitting head down with my elbows on my desk and the ball of my hands placed just above my ears. This was the optimal position to give my fingers freedom to scratch the dandruff off my scalp. I could then distract myself by moulding the resulting small white piles of dead skin into an endless array of interesting shapes. Desperate times required desperate measures.

Despite this mental torture I sailed through my 11 Plus and secured a place at a not-so-local Convent Grammar School for Young Ladies. While not exactly a match made in Heaven—there was no question of me being allowed to play football or wear trousers—it was a great place to learn.

I guess I must have immediately stood out as a bit different. Firstly, my parents guilted me into wearing the hideous brown corduroy hat which they had purchased at enormous expense, despite the advice of the sales assistants in the John Lewis School Uniform department. Clearly aware that I was heading for unnecessary ridicule, I recall one prim lady telling Mum and Dad that the uniform list was out of date, and the hat hadn't been a mandatory item of clothing since before the outbreak of the second World War. But no, it was on the list so we bought it, and I wore it. Uncool. Another reason I stood out related to my size—I was a large eleven-year-old. I had pretty much completed my vertical growth by then, and I remember wondering why my class included so many children of kindergarten age. For their part, I'm sure they were surprised that a 6th Former had been relegated to Year 7, and out of respect or pity voted me in as their first class prefect.

Life at Bellerive was good. I quickly established myself as a regular choice in the netball team—my height combined with lack of mobility making Goal Shooter the perfect position. Success in tennis and rounders followed. I continued to excel in maths, and launched myself fully into the previously unexplored joys of physics and chemistry. So there were lots of positives. However, I was a long way short of being an academically gifted all-rounder, as there were many areas in which I'm sure I proved to be a great disappointment to parents and teachers alike.

Musically I registered somewhere at the low end of the scale between F and utterly useless. I don't know how long I endured the agony of private violin lessons eating away at my Saturday mornings – I guess it went on for two years. But I distinctly remember the joyous day when—in an act of outright rebellion fuelled by my newly acquired status as a teenager—I lay down my bow for the final time. My happiness lasted just as long as it took for the same bow to be picked up enthusiastically by my equally unmusical father. With his typical 'can do' attitude he took over my lessons then proceeded to spend every free moment of the rest of his long life reminding me that bad things happen to those who quit. To be fair to Dad, the Tuneless Violin Torture didn't last much longer than a decade, after which I had moved out of hearing range (180 miles) of the source of the torment, and he had improved to a level where he was invited to play in local orchestras.

Languages didn't go down too well with me either. Despite my best efforts, French, Spanish and Latin were all foreign to me. Especially Latin. It didn't help that the subject was taught by a spinster who was a second cousin of the mad emperor Nero, and had emerged unscathed from the sacking of Rome. Her lessons comprised of endless repetition of '*amo, amas, amat, amamus, amatis, amant*', which—thanks to Google—I now know to be the first conjugation of the verb 'to love'.

Art? Yes, rubbish at that as well—unless I could count my exquisite, innovative designs of football kits. Designs that were unthinkable in the days when all goalkeepers wore green, referees wore black, and dual-colour stripes were as exciting as it got. Sadly, this was not considered an acceptable subject for my O-Level portfolio. Neither was my love of Dennis Wheatley, whose stories of the occult captured my interest far more than the literary classics that formed my O-Level English Literature syllabus. But what I lacked in natural talent, I more than made up for in sheer hard work. I worked my socks off to get good exam results; evenings, weekends, holidays—all regularly sacrificed at the altar of study and revision.

Religion? Well that's an interesting one. I was born into a Catholic family (Dad converted soon after marrying Mum—now that's true love) and attended Catholic schools until I was 18. However, I stopped believing in God around the same time I realised that Santa and the Tooth Fairy were just harmless stories parents told their children to add magic and discipline to life. Incidentally, this happened long before I thought to question Mum's Eastern European ancestry, or discovered the embarrassing truth that *welligogs* was not a word commonly used to describe waterproof boots. I was well into my 20s when that mistake was corrected.

From a young age I couldn't get my tiny—but logical—brain around why an allegedly kind, loving and all-powerful God couldn't (or wouldn't) allow babies who died before being baptised to join him immediately in Heaven. Why would he insist on sending them to an unpleasant staging post called Purgatory? Why would he subject them to a process to cleanse them of their sin? How long did it take? What did he do to them while they were there? WHAT POSSIBLE SIN COULD A NEWBORN INFANT BE GUILTY OF? Then there was the question of why he CHOSE to allow a mother to carry her baby for 9 long months, just to take it away from her at the very end. This was the behaviour of a psychopath, NOT the kind and loving father his Public Relations team made him out to be.

These were just a few of a myriad of questions that troubled me. I was also profoundly concerned for my non-Catholic grandparents who hadn't converted to Catholicism when my parents married. They were wonderful people who seemed destined for an afterlife fighting the Devil in the fires of Hell. FOR ETERNITY. I don't recall if this made me sad, angry or both. As with my questions about Purgatory, I was always fobbed off with implausible responses. That, and a crystal clear message that if I kept making such enquiries, I would suffer the wrath of the Almighty. So I stopped asking and assumed it was all just another elaborate fib, albeit far more disturbing and cruel than the others. I played along just enough to ensure I didn't ruffle too many feathers and get myself thrown out of school.

Even before I stopped believing, Sunday Mass was a battleground where my brother and I would use our enforced proximity to entertain ourselves by kicking and punching each other, until our parents gave up in exasperation and moved one of us to a dark corner of the church. With the welcome distraction of pain and physical violence now gone, and the constant stand up, sit down, do the hokey cokey that accompanies Catholic Mass making trips to my personal virtual universe impractical (more about this magical place later), the rest of the service passed by at an agonisingly slow pace, until the priest spoke the eagerly awaited words 'the mass is over, go in peace'. I stopped listening at the word 'over' and demonstrated unusual speed and agility to be first out the door ready to resume sibling hostilities.

On the social side of school life, I was undoubtedly held back by my parents' evening-class arrangements, which prevented me from engaging fully in the Friday morning conversations centred on the previous day's edition of *Top of the Pops*. At 5.30pm on Thursdays child care responsibility was abdicated to a set of grandparents, allowing Mum to escape to Spanish class while Dad continued to perfect his Karate skills—a sport I believed he had taken up as an essential defence against my evil brother. It would appear that this was another fabrication of my disturbed mind. Unfortunately for me the grandparents who looked after us were avid followers of Coronation Street, a programme that aired at exactly the same time as Top of the Pops. To this day I tense up the moment I hear the distinctive 'derrrr de de de de derr' that introduces the theme tune of my most hated program.

I did my best to compensate for the loss of Top of the Pops through the weekly purchase of Jackie or other such magazine that consumed the conversation of my teenage classmates. Occasionally I even read it. At least I read the sections that related to music.

Sections about fashion, makeup and boys never got more than a cursory glance. The effort and expense paid dividends though, as it allowed me to actively engage in discussions on the relative merits of the Bay City Rollers verses Donny Osmond verses David Cassidy. For the record, I couldn't stand the clean cut Donny Osmond or any of his assortment of siblings. David Cassidy was OK, but it was the Bay City Rollers whose music and general scruffiness got my vote. Hidden beneath this outward display of normal teenage girl musical taste was a much stronger preference for the music played by Phil Easton on Radio City's Great Easton Express. Music such as *You Can Go to Hell* by Alice Cooper (my first single, flip side *Feed My Frankenstein*). Music that was discussed not in the classrooms of teenage girls, but by boys in 6th Form common rooms. Boys such as my brother, who by this stage was engaging in a whole new and experimental range of rebellious activities. Activities such as painting his entire bedroom—walls, ceiling, woodwork, furniture — using a palette of paints limited to matt black and dark purple. Maybe—just maybe—there was hope for our relationship.

Whilst Jackie served as a useful display of normalness, my real interest lay in the publication Mum picked up from the newsagents every Monday morning for 112 weeks. Each one resulted in the temporary suspension of her parental duties as she locked herself away in the kitchen. Once settled, she expertly tuned out the screams of her bickering children, and indulged in a few hours of undisturbed pleasure. When her time was up, she emerged serenely from her sanctuary, and carefully placed the magazine in one of the 7 elegant binders that took pride of place on the bookshelf. The title of the series that so fascinated myself and Mum was *Man, Myth & Magic: An Illustrated Encyclopaedia of the Supernatural.* It included mesmerising articles from respected scientists on subjects such as spontaneous human combustion, the Bermuda Triangle and Claudia, a girl who could turn tennis balls inside out with just the power of her mind. Oh, how I longed to master that particular party trick.

My youthful nerdiness and general innocence ensured that

I was a late arrival at the Table of Real-Life Knowledge. One notable example of my naivety was when Sister Mary Gabriel, the headmistress, proceeded to inform the entire school about the building work that had just started. 'Now girls,' she started in her most soothing Irish lilt, 'you will have noticed that builders have taken over one corner of the playground, and have begun to put up scaffolding. It will be extremely dangerous over there, so *I must insist* that no one goes near the builders' erection.' Only myself and Sister Mary Gabriel didn't understand why this sensible Health and Safety precaution triggered such hilarity among the massed rank of girls and hastily stifled giggles among the staff.

I spent many hours of my young life inhabiting a parallel universe of my own invention, in a state commonly known as day dreaming. I could transport myself into this universe at will, and the mind numbing tedium of history lessons was a frequent trigger for the journey. What I liked most about my universe was that the simple command 'Beam me up Scottie' could instantly take me anywhere I wanted to go. Virtual travel options were limited only by my imagination. My preferred destinations often corresponded to locations linked to recent editions of Man, Myth & Magic. Amongst my favourite activities was scuba diving in the Bermuda Triangle, where I would locate another missing aircraft by following in the wake of a helpful pod of dolphins. Another regular destination was Peru. It was here that a slim and fit version of myself could be found effortlessly climbing the slopes of Machu Picchu while exploring the lost world of the Incas.

Although entering my alternative reality was easy enough, leaving for the return journey was a much greater challenge. More often than not, exit through the departure lounge required a sudden jolt—such as that caused by the rapid coming together of my head and my desk. Alternatively, the contact of a well-targeted board duster or a piece of chalk would have the same effect. Back then teachers could throw whatever they liked at their pupils with impunity.

Now may be a good time to rewind a little and clear up the confusion over my father's occupation. It came about because those who created the English language were either too stubborn or too lazy to agree on a unique definition of the noun *plant*. My father was a member of the Institute of Plant Engineers. Obviously I associated his work with that of Bill Masen, the hero of the John Wyndham book *The Day of The Triffids*. For the benefit of those whose knowledge of 1950s sci-fi is sketchy, triffids were kick-ass, venomous plants that could move, communicate and consign anyone who caused them even the most minor irritation to a grisly death. Bill Masen—who fortunately survived an acid attack with only superficial burns—took on the job of saving mankind from these terrifying monsters that were believed to be the product of Russian bio-engineering. So there you have it. Bill Masen and my father were both Plant Engineers.

Seriously, how was I supposed to know the same word can also mean *machinery*? What's wrong with the Institute of Machinery Engineers? Nada. Nothing. Call a spade a spade for heaven's sake. I felt a great sense of injustice when I learned that it was this more mundane type of plant that Dad lovingly tended when he left home for his job at the Fords car factory.

As far back as my early childhood, I had shown a real flair for inventions involving advanced engineering concepts. I was probably no older than 5 when I designed my first Santa alarm—a masterpiece of pulleys, levers and counterweights. Its purpose was to make sure that if I fell asleep on Christmas Eve, I would let go of the string I was holding. This would result in a large pile of books being dropped from height into my dolls' pram[3], and the ensuing noise would surely be enough to jolt me back into complete wakefulness. The device worked to perfection, except that I underestimated the decibel level required to wake an exhausted 5-year-old. A rookie mistake.

3 Just in case you're worried, no dolls were hurt. They were all removed from the line of fire and spent the night cosied up with me in bed.

Despite this early promise, I never developed a true love of engineering. Unlike my brother, I had no interest in building model planes and leaving signature pools of immovable balsa cement dispersed across the dinner table. Neither did I yearn to go out in all weathers to fly the creations around desolate fields, smash them into a gazillion pieces then start the painstaking process of putting them back together. I wasn't devoid of practical skills though, and I performed minor fixes on my first car. I was adept at routine tasks such as changing spark plugs, adjusting tappets, tightening fan belts, and I even replaced a broken fan belt with a pair of tights. But a grease monkey I was not. Another flaw that held me back was my scant regard for the excess nuts and bolts that inexplicably remained at the end of most of my jobs.

The same level of thought went into selecting my career as had gone into my choice of A-level subjects. Very little. Although I considered the option of medicine, I soon realised that even if I had been intelligent enough (which I wasn't), my undignified squeamishness in the presence of blood would be problematic. Instead, I chose to follow in the footsteps of both my father and brother, and become an engineer. It was this family history of engineering, together with the fact I was good at physics and maths that convinced myself, my parents and my career officer that this was the perfect career choice.

I was fortunate to be entering the profession at a time when the Government was pumping vast quantities of money into engineering apprenticeships and actively encouraging girls to apply. Without the assistance of my dear friend, Positive Discrimination, I doubt I would have got far in my interview with Rolls Royce in Bristol[4]. Everyone knows Rolls Royce makes cars, but I was completely unaware they also manufactured turbine engines for many of the world's major aircraft companies. In my defence, this was before the Internet came along to make background research a synch. If either of the male engineers in the family knew Rolls Royce had

4 Shortly after starting at Rolls Royce, I picked up the nickname Rachel—as in Rachel Discrimination.

an Engine Division, they didn't think it worthy of mention. But fortune was on my side, and this oversight did not prevent me from securing an apprenticeship, along with a place at the University of Bath to study Mechanical Engineering.

So what was student life like for early members of Generation X? Well, I was certainly not alone in being flush with cash from an engineering apprenticeship, supplemented by a generous maintenance grant. Extremely cheap beer was easy to find, accommodation was inexpensive and came with free cakes (I lived above a rather excellent bakery), and there were no tuition fees to pay back. Life on campus revolved around the bar and sports hall, with just occasional visits to the library and lecture theatres. Off campus there was an amazing range of pubs, both within the confines of Bath city centre, and the surrounding countryside. Pubs where I encountered my first (of many) pints of Somerset scrumpy, learned the useful life skills of playing bar billiards and shove ha'penny, and listened to music from a juke box that contained such magical tracks as *Whiter Shade of Pale* by Procul Harem, and Led Zepplin's *Stairway to Heaven*.

I must have done some work, it's just that I honestly don't remember when—or indeed what. It wasn't until my final year that I realised degrees were awarded with different classifications; from First Class through two flavours of Second Class then bottoming out at Third Class—which I understood to be a kinder way to describe Failure Class. I might have misread the situation, but I don't recall that anyone cared too much what level they got (as long as it was above a Third). Or at least they didn't care enough to pull more than the occasional all-night study session. So yes, student life was easy. Sorry Millennials, I suspect this is not what you want to hear right now. Especially not from a member of the generation that described you—in no less a publication than *Time Magazine*—as a bunch of 'lazy, entitled, narcissists'.

Oh and here's another uncomfortable truth. Back then the entry requirements were so much lower than today. My offer of a place was dependent upon achieving nothing more demanding in my A-levels than 2 B grades and a C. Even though I fell short of that lowly target I was still welcomed with open arms. I raise this not with any desire to rub more salt in open wounds, but because it throws light on another reason why Millennials are under so much pressure—life is so much more competitive now.

2

Harriet

Mum has done a great job of describing my childhood years so I won't add much. She explains that I gave up tennis because of the physical damage it was going to my body. However, my recollection is that I stopped playing tennis because I asked to; even as a ten-year-old, I could sense that the tennis environment was full of politics and tension, and I didn't want to be a part of it any longer. When I asked her if I could stop, she responded with 'Well you have to do another sport otherwise you'll get fat', and so I became a badminton player.

When she asked me to read her book and write my own chapter, I had no preconceived idea of what I would say. So when I read it in full one day, I just started writing, and this is the (edited) result. I often write down my own feelings as it helps me make sense of them and the events which led me to them. I write a chronological story of the previous few days of my life, ending in the crux of my problem and hopefully a solution. This writing style has persisted here, but documenting a much longer time frame, as it is probably the only way to truly understand the thoughts and decisions that resulted in my current life choices. Life choices which partly triggered my mum to write this incredible book and share her experience of being the mother of millennials. Here goes.

Besides two years of depression between sixteen and eighteen years old, I had lived nineteen years of a happy life. I had a huge network of friends, was always supported, praised, achieving, seizing every opportunity I could, and being far too independent. The safety net of schools and structure prepared me for university where I did well, but on completion of my degree I decided to leave education and enter the world of work. I mentioned that I had lived happily for nineteen years because in my twentieth year I met my first and only (so far) boyfriend. I have no idea if he intended to treat me the way he did, or whether he knew the full extent of the damage his behaviour was doing to me. But I believe there were numerous times when he abused me; verbally, emotionally and physically. Looking back, I feel he took advantage of my good nature and naivety, and over a period of three years made me a fraction of the person I really was.

We stayed together until I realised I was numb. It would be a relief if I left a friend's house and I had managed to feign enough interest to hold a conversation. A series of events led to me realising our relationship had to end, and I immediately regained and relished in my independence. I had the most blissful and invigorating six months in Bristol, during which time I realised how much I was underselling myself at work. The job just wasn't good enough for me and my potential. I applied for a Graduate Scheme which was run in Universities and charities all over the country, and I was selected to work at the University of Cambridge.

I was initially hesitant as it was so far away and I didn't know anyone there, but I knew I'd make friends as I'm so sociable. The institution was perceived as prestigious, and everyone kept saying 'It will look so good on your CV', so I took the job and moved there in late August. Within two weeks I was unhappy. I felt like I had put on loads of weight for no reason and I was often welling up, something I hadn't experienced since being in my last relationship. On my first trip home, my doctor diagnosed me with stress-induced Irritable Bowel Syndrome. This shocked me because I didn't know stress could have such a profound physical effect on your body. But I was also comforted by the diagnosis as it reduced the confusion and blame I was placing on myself.

On my return to Cambridge, I referred myself to the university counselling service and began counselling a few weeks later. To my surprise, what I thought would be the main topic of conversation- my long-term body issues- turned into acknowledging the sudden and immense loss of my sense of belonging, caused by moving to Cambridge. In addition, counselling helped me begin to understand the hang ups and triggers of my previous relationship. Armed with new information about myself, I started to get mentally better. Not everything improved though—there's only so much you can achieve with 10 hours of counselling. My fear of failure remained, as did a deep-rooted desire for continued achievement (in this case in the form of a career), and I continued to show commitment to others at the detriment of myself.

At the start of 2017 I finally thought I'd carved a life for myself out of this boring and characterless place. But then my job – the sole reason for moving and making most aspects of my life worse – fell apart and continued to do so until the end of my contract in August. It was far too much of a gradual and subtle process to explain here, but essentially I felt completely disregarded, neglected and undervalued. This resulted in me wasting my time and talents, and the job certainly wasn't rewarding the loyalty and sacrifices I had made to be there. I went about trying to solve the problem as professionally and stoically as I could, but my efforts were never fulfilled. Failing after failing led to me regularly crying on my cycle into work, having to spend an hour in the park composing myself, and crying down the phone to my friends or in front of colleagues.

One day in May, I had finished working at an event in London I had co-organised. I should have been proud and happy, but I couldn't shake a bad mood. Even after sitting in gorgeously sunny London parks, and catching up with a few friends, I knew I was too unhappy. I made the decision that I wouldn't even attempt to get another job in Cambridge, and would move back to Bristol as soon as the contract was over. This decision reduced the pressure for a while, but I still expected to carry on in this field of work on my return home. Unfortunately, the failings and neglect I continued to experience made me not want to—or even think my health would allow me to—explore another office job. It felt like I'd wasted a year of my life being miserable. I began to toy with the idea of travelling as I had money saved, and a friend who was going through similar professional frustrations. The time came to leave Cambridge. I said my goodbyes to the people I cared about then drove home the moment I could stuff all my belongings into my car.

Life was blissful for a month; I was back in my usual social groups, it was gloriously sunny, I started playing good badminton again, and I took the time to relax. I went to Bali for two weeks with friends, had a blast, and it got me seriously thinking about travelling, as I knew I still wasn't ready for work. The day I got back from Bali, I met a friend in London and we booked a bunch of flights. No going back now, we were going to Australia, New Zealand, Fiji, and South America.

I spent another month in Bristol planning and preparing, but I remember often feeling quite lost during this time. Besides travelling, I had no idea what I wanted to do, or how best to utilise my talents—and not disappoint myself and those around me. The day came, we flew to the other side of the world. Despite being sick for a week in Peru and missing Machu Picchu, I had the most incredible three months of my life. I had countless unforgettable experiences, met some amazing people, and realised that doing what you want every day—be it reading in the park, or staring at New Zealand landscapes out of a coach window—made me so much happier and stress free. Compared to my earlier life where I always trying to impress people with my work, and being sucked into a toxic environment full of ego, injustice and politics—a no brainer, really!

During my time away, a number of key things happened which set me on my current path; I put in my application for an office job and felt only relief when I didn't get accepted; I jumped out of a plane and understood that the temporary fear of something is nothing compared to the exhilaration and permanent sense of achievement it can bring; a conversation on a sail boat with a traveller whose dad was a carpenter, put the idea of doing a woodworking course in my head; I met a stranger on a park bench who told me that the way I spoke about painting filled her with excitement, and was starkly different to the way I spoke about my past work; and finally, I visited possibly the purest place on earth: Gaiatree.

Gaiatree is a sanctuary on an island in Fiji called Taveuni, owned by two incredible people who had dreams, a good internet connection, and belief in themselves. They spent years creating a paradise of nature, beautiful food and cyclone-proof concrete domes (with a little help from YouTube videos). I was so inspired by their bravery and calm dedication that my mind was made up. Once I returned home I was not going back to work, instead I would explore my creative side and build something that is entirely mine. I make the rules. I succeed. I fail. I can finally be proud of myself.

After another month in South America, I came home and started cracking on with my dream; I adored woodworking, would get lost in painting for hours on end, and spent every evening with friends doing something fun. I was, and still am, incredibly happy. Since my return home, I have embarked on my 're-education' in an attempt to create a varied career which uses the multitude of skills I already possess, and encourages me to learn more *for myself*, not just because it will look good on my CV. In the words of Emilie Wapnick in her Ted Talk, I'm a *multipotentialite*, and I feel fortunate to be working on several projects which better utilise my range of skills. I have never felt more fulfilled, proud, and confident in myself.

I am speaking for myself here—based on twenty-five years of my personal experience, association and opportunities, which no one else will have gone through in the same way. I don't believe that office environments are bad for everyone, and as my mum points out, perhaps it's the lingering doctrine of older generations that allows people to 'just get on with it'. That, and a host of different mental capabilities, perspectives and priorities in life. But the Millennial movement seems to highlight a need for significantly different outcomes from work. Especially when considering the exponential growth in job opportunities not previously stated on any career test, and the predominance of mental health issues which are afflicting young people everywhere.

Yet we are still being educated in a manner, so entrenched in social norms, that mould us into believing we need to spend our lives working for other people, and steadily progressing until you're the one other people are working for. Never was I told that you could work for yourself! We study an array of subjects, we get graded on them, we build our educational profile, all in the mindset that it will be utilised by, and for someone else. We then start working for someone else who, understandably, will never put your best interest above their own or that of the company. Often causing the hard work, loyalty, and pride you placed on your achievements to become diluted, and only validated when recognised by someone above your pay grade.

I believe that if business and entrepreneurship was taught alongside all topics at school—to better inspire children with a sense of autonomy—the things that could come from their brains and imagination would be massive. And perhaps they would come to fruition much earlier than if they've dulled part of themselves trying to be a big fish in a huge ocean, full of predatory beasts and toxic waste.

A subject area I have recently been pondering, is my reluctance to assign myself to typical gender norm. My sporting achievements from a young age made me believe there was no substantial difference between boys and girls; my academic achievements were stellar; I also chose the fashion of boys for many years whilst at primary school—the photos are hilarious. I've led my life being above average in everything, and therefore never seeing myself as less than anyone else. In fact, the only times I have experienced overt sexism is at badminton clubs, when older men don't let me knock up with them. So I get on a different court and feel proud and smug as they look on in surprise that I'm 'far better than a girl should be'.

So all my life, I've been who and what I thought I wanted to be. I get to university, study hard and obtain so many extra-curricular merits that I'm as good a future employee as you could imagine. Since you can't do a Psychology-specific job with just a BSc in Psychology, you have to branch out. So while at university I attended countless CV workshops and career advice sessions to help me decide my next step. Unfortunately, no one told me that you shouldn't just apply for jobs where you can already do everything, and that it's okay to have gaps in your knowledge and experience.

This was such a monumental flaw in my thinking, that the first job I applied for, I did so because I could already do everything on the job description. The same thing happened when I applied for the Graduate Scheme. It wasn't until a respected peer advised me to only go for jobs where you can do 2/3rds, half at a push, of what is stated on the job description; it's as much about you learning new skills from that job, as it is for the company to get value from you. I was quite disheartened by this knowledge, as it confirmed my suspicions that I had been short-selling, and therefore short-changing myself for 3 years. I vowed to take on that advice for my next application.

I also didn't realise how common this trend is for girls, which helped me understand why several of my guy friends were in weird and wonderful jobs that had nothing to do with their degrees and paid quite handsomely. They literally had the balls to apply to stuff. I'm kind of angry at myself—someone who has never viewed being a girl as a weakness, accidentally slotting straight into a harmful statistic. One day I'm going to experiment, and apply to a bunch of well-paid jobs that I don't have the right skills for, and see if my new-found confidence can wangle me a hire.

To anyone who reads this book, please tell all the girls you know to avoid the mistake that I made. Tell them to have confidence in themselves and their skills. Explain that their priority should be the value something can add to their life, not what they can add to something or someone else.

When I decided not go back to 'work', and instead explore my own project, one of the hardest aspects about this was the loss of perceived status; having to say 'I live with my parents' faces a certain judgement in your mid-twenties. When saying 'I don't have a job, I'm trying to set up my own business', I can't help but cringe at what people think, because this approach is so far from what I have been educated for and find comfortable. But I know for certain, that although saying these things is hard, doing them makes me very happy, and fortunately that overrides any perceived negative judgement. I love living at home, seeing my dog all day, then my parents in the evening. I love the house now everyone is making the effort to keep it tidy, and I have all the tools and space to explore my art project. I'm incredibly lucky to have landed in this scenario, with this opportunity.

Cambridge was such a bad year for me I have made the decision that I won't be loyal to someone else, another company, another set of social norms. Instead, I'm taking that year back and being loyal to myself and prioritising my health and happiness. I am now appreciative of the time I had there; I learnt a lot, made some great friends, and all the negativity and hurt I endured resulted in a journey which has led to months of continued self-discovery, increased confidence, and a better understanding of my passions as well as the things that I don't want in my life. I feel calmer and look at negative situations in a very different light; they won't last forever if you're proactive about changing them, and you will learn a lot from them. Ultimately they will help you navigate your way through the rest of your life.

These negative situations help you find your necessary life variables; the key aspects which you need in order to live in a sustained happy state. Moving to Cambridge—and living a starkly different life to what I had in Bristol—highlighted the variables I most need in my life at the moment. I need to be close to my friends and engage in a level of sociability which fuels my extroversion. I need to pursue my hobbies—namely badminton and painting—to an appropriate level, as these maintain and increase my self-esteem and help me relax.

On a par with the importance of the people around me, is

the importance of my environment. Cambridge is undeniably a beautiful city, but the town centre closes at 6pm. Besides going to the pub and drinking, I encountered no sense of community or fun. Bristol has spoiled me with expecting vibrancy around every corner and a steady stream of eclectic strangers, which makes it because it's a city that facilitates you to be yourself and find your people. My workplace environment also needs to invoke a sense of justice and respect for everyone. I now know I have the responsibility to maintain these variables and stay attuned to when they are not being fulfilled, or when the variables themselves change as I evolve.

A twenty-five year long road trip, with many seemingly small and insignificant events, has resulted in my arrival at this point. I personally don't believe that anything happens for a reason because I don't know what the 'reason' is. But I do believe that if you are at a point where you want—or feel the need—for something to change, you might just come across the catalysts if you keep your eyes and ears open. I have well and truly gone through my *quarter life crisis*, from which I have come out the other end a happier and more confident person[5]. If I could impart any advice on someone it would be thus:

There will probably come a time—or many—when nothing seems to go right, you feel lost, sad, numb. There is nothing wrong with those feelings, nothing wrong with crying, or asking for help. But it is only temporary, and it is probably your body's way of showing you that you need to change something. Don't be afraid of that change and take the time to reflect on your feelings to discover what your body and mind might be yearning for.

Or more poetically: *'It's a dangerous business, Frodo, going out your door. You step onto the road, and if you don't keep your feet, there's no knowing where you might be swept off to.'* J.R.R. Tolkien.

5 I have continued to pursue my creative side and am now an independent artist, creating wooden canvasses out of recycled wood and hand painting them with designs depicting the vibrancy and beauty of nature. You can find my work on Instagram @paintandgrainbristol. Alongside this, I have furthered my passion for badminton and become a coach to a range of ages and abilities across Bristol, imparting onto others my knowledge and enthusiasm for the sport I love.

Sally #MyChapter

Hello everyone, it is I, The Great Sally! Haha, I'm just kidding. That's just a false bravado I've managed to conjure up to hide my massive anxiety about writing and sharing my life. There are a lot of things I would like to talk about here, and many things I don't. This chapter is my chance to give people a brief glimpse of what my life was like while I was growing up, and how it shaped me in to the person I am today. I'm sure my mum has already told you loads, but I saw things from a different perspective, one I will try my best to share with you here.

How about starting off with the things that are the most prominent in my life – my mental health problems. I've been to therapists and doctors and have been diagnosed with depression, anxiety and PTSD (Post Traumatic Stress Disorder). I also believe I have the symptoms of C-PTSD (Complex PTSD), but I'll explain more about that shortly.

I've had depression for what feels like my whole life – my earliest memories are those of me being overwhelmed and distressed. Starting from nursery (maybe even before then) until now, there has definitely been a theme. I've always felt distinctly different from everyone, and I've always wanted to be. I felt very alone, desperate for connection. Looking back now I think this stems from having a lack of connection with my parents. I don't blame anyone for this, my parents really loved me, and always wanted the best for me. But

I was a sensitive individual, and I had deeper needs that they didn't realise they had to support. I remember once when I was young, I suddenly became overwhelmed with sadness. I didn't know why I was so distressed, so I did what I always did to cheer myself up. I went to mummy. She gave me a hug and asked me why I was crying. I told her I didn't know. She looked irritated and confused and told me 'people don't cry for no reason'.

'People don't cry for no reason' really resonated with me. I started thinking. So why do I get sad all the time? Is there something wrong with me? Why am I like this? Mum doesn't understand, I can't talk to her about this. If I can't talk to Mum, I can't talk to anyone.

So I didn't. From then on through the remainder of primary school, I figured out ways to hide it. Loads of things happened that I would love to write down and share with you, but if I start talking too much, I'll end up writing a book of my own...;)

Want to find out about my book? Catch up with the latest news here.

So yeah, I've been depressed for as long as I can remember, and I started to show symptoms of mild anxiety in secondary school. I believe it was a gradual development over time, due to the ongoing yet low-key bullying, or what the lads tried to disguise as 'banter'. I was a weird child, I didn't exactly have an eye for fashion, and I was really shy. Thankfully I found friends who were kind of weird too. We worked well together, and we learnt how to be more normal. My best friend was the only reason I survived going to school every day. She always managed to keep me upbeat. From what I remember it was a long time before we even talked about my depression, but that didn't matter because we were always there for each other. Then she left to study at a different sixth form, and so did the majority of my other close friends.

I was alone with a bunch of people I didn't really connect with, and others I felt genuine discomfort to be around. I felt as though I was a giant turd walking into an industrial-sized fan. These people fed off gossip, and I tended to be their food source. The stress of the world began to crush me, and one day it felt like I just stopped working. Maybe it was the new anti-depressants I was on, or maybe I was holding so much inside me that I became numb.

At first I actually enjoyed studying – chemistry especially. We had the best teacher, he was the only one who wouldn't let me sleep in class. Although, looking back, I'm not sure if staying awake was actually a good thing—I had slept through most of my earlier school life, and got amazing GCSEs.

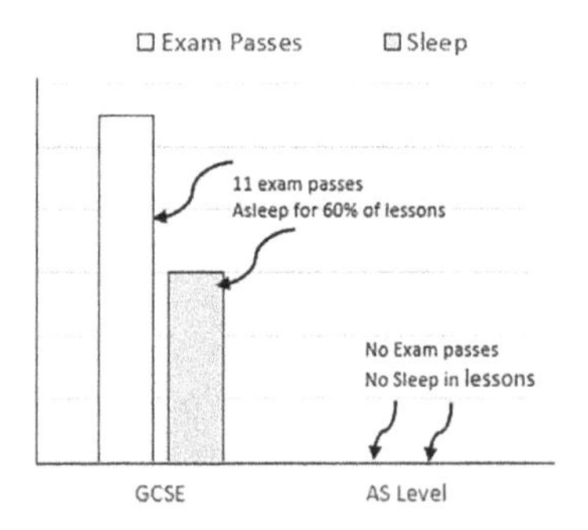

Exam Success vs Sleep in Lessons

I'm sure you'll agree there appears to be a pretty strong correlation here. (And yes I know correlation ≠ causation, it's only a joke.)

So I had finally found a subject which was genuinely fascinating, and a teacher who always wanted to make sure I was on board. But it soon felt as though we had way too much to learn, too quickly. And without my best friend to talk through the homework with,

I started to lose my momentum. By the end of the year my brain felt thoroughly stuffed with pieces of hastily learnt and misremembered information. Nothing else seemed to be going in, and I couldn't piece together what was already there. I dropped out of two exams and really struggled to make it to my others. My results came back when I was having an already bad day in Botswana (more about that another time). There was no chance of continuing my education with those grades.

I dropped out. I. Dropped. Out. WTF. I didn't know where to go from there. It felt like I'd just fallen off the conveyor belt and I'd gotten lost in the land below. At least I had a boyfriend, who I ended up spending loads of time with. But nothing lasts forever and sometimes that's for the best. I managed to get a temporary Christmas job and started talking about my next steps. Of course my mum and I were both desperate to continue my education, because what am I unless I'm smart? What future could I possibly have without a degree? Life was getting increasingly stressful, but I was determined to soldier on. Thankfully a beautiful dog came into my life and helped me feel slightly more grounded. He gave me cuddles and kisses when I needed them. With the help of my newest friend and all the kisses from the goodest boy, I was able to keep my head above water.

I met a new boyfriend as I was just starting a new job, I was learning to drive and I was getting ready to go to college. If I was keeping my head above water before, this guy was #MyLifejacket. Things were going pretty well. I was predicted to get the highest grade for the course, and I found the content quite easy. Part of the Animal Management course involved work experience which for some reason I chose to do in a dog groomers on the other side of the city. It was hard work, but it started looking like I might have another chance.

That's when my life came screeching to a halt once again. For now I'm just going to say a *traumatic event* occurred, and suddenly I was no longer able to function. I struggle to remember the months after the incident. According to my mum and boyfriend, I spent most of this time crying, gaming and sleeping. Emphasis on the sleeping. I would sleep all day if I could. Once I had been asleep the whole day. Mum tried to wake me but I was out cold. I could see how frightened she was when she finally shook me awake, terrified that maybe I had tried to end it. I was pretty much unable to function, for months I was in a constant and debilitating depression. Even with expensive weekly therapy, I was struggling to get my head back into reality. I quit my job, my work experience and I would have quit college if it weren't for my friends and a few good teachers who helped me barely scrape a pass.

Sometime during the months that followed I was diagnosed with PTSD, and later found a technique that helped to reduce my flashbacks – both their frequency and intensity. I realised that my flashbacks to the *traumatic event* were similar to those I regularly experienced from moments in my childhood. I read something on Facebook about C-PTSD and started to connect the dots. With the information I have gathered, I conclude the most likely explanation to be as follows: I was a sensitive child who experienced a mild version of CEN (Childhood Emotional Neglect). I developed C-PTSD from a combination of the mildly traumatic experiences I was constantly exposed to, and the *traumatic event*. The depression probably didn't help.

After a long time readjusting to reality (and gaining a few stone), I was able to start slowly moving forwards again. Unfortunately I was still stuck on the idea that the only way to progress was by putting myself through more education and work experience. And so my life became about dogs. I was doing dog behaviour courses and set up a doggy day care business with my mum. I loved it! I love dogs, how couldn't you? They're just adorable fluffy balls of unconditional love. Except when they're not. Except when they're escaping from their harnesses. Except when they have your own dog's neck firmly stuck between their jaws.

My depression was getting worse, and this job was causing more stress than I realised. I started falling back into my constant crying and sleeping habits. This went on for about a year. Then while I was on holiday with my boyfriend it became clear I couldn't put myself back into that situation. The hardest part was letting my mum down. This was the plan for my future! And I couldn't hack it. At least some inspiration from a friend gave me an alternative to suggest – I would start studying A-level chemistry from home.

All my life my experiences have been shaping me as a person, and I barely even realised it. Every time someone said something negative, whether it was a joke or not, their words would latch on and cling to my own self-worth. My guard is up too much. Constantly being friends with people who didn't 'get me', or took advantage of me, has really affected how I see the world now. I avoid strangers at all costs, to me it feels like everyone would hurt me if I gave them the chance. I hate leaving the house alone or even worse, going to town on my own. I'll only go if I desperately need to. I'm scared people will hurt me, but mostly I'm scared of bumping into someone from my past. I push my new friends away so they can't do it to me, and I hide away in the house trying not to think about anything. But I ended up having far too much to think about.

It took me a long time to piece everything together, and I managed to do it with the help of social media. Facebook in particular. Facebook used to be an unhealthy place for me to spend my time. It used to be full of the pretty people having fun, and of my friends going to parties without me. It used to be a place of comparison and resentment, yet I would continue to go there for hours each day, trying to make it seem like I too had an amazing life. It wasn't until I was 20 years old when I decided to change that. At this point I had around 600 'friends' on Facebook. They were mostly people from school, and therefore mostly people I did not like. One day I was sick of seeing my actual friends still being buddies with the guy that subjected me to the *traumatic event* (yeh, I was raped), and I got desperate. I deleted a few people as friends (and so from my life) and it felt pretty good. I deleted a few more, and more until I had eliminated roughly 400 people. I no longer had to follow these people's lives and they could no longer snoop on mine (well they could, but now with a little less ease).

It didn't take long for my news feed to start filling up with things I actually wanted to see. My mood and quality of life slowly improved, and over time I gradually began to learn more about myself. And then Facebook did something awesome. With a feature that many people are scared of, Facebook started to know me better than I did myself. I was doing my normal scrolling one day when I came across a promoted page. One that I didn't yet follow, but that Facebook 'thinks' I might enjoy. This page helped to put the word *empath* into my vocabulary. It wasn't a big deal for me when I found it, because it was just a label that described my 'symptoms'. I didn't feel like having a word for it would really change anything. But as soon as I told my mum, she almost jumped out of her seat with excitement. By using this label and explaining what it meant, I helped my mum to understand me in a way she never could before.

She went on to buy us both a copy of *The Empath Survival Guide*, and so began the semi-spiritual journey that I am currently – and probably always will be – taking. There's more about this in Chapter 7, *An Empath in the Family.*

Facebook also started showing me articles about PTSD, C-PTSD, CEN, Depression and Anxiety, but all in a more scientific and focused way than before. I used to get links such as 'What kind of vegetable are you?' but now I get articles about mental health that are based on real science. Even YouTube has thrown some eye-opening videos at me. People are often scared of the power of social media, and how much these platforms know about their users… you'd be stupid not to. But if you use it to your advantage, it seems, you can learn more about yourself than you would have expected.

There was still a cloud of depression over my every moment, and now I had much more time on my hands. I was still getting therapy which was helpful, but more in the long term than in the short. I delved into the world of Old School Runescape, a game that I used to play when I was younger. I played that game for days straight, my xp gains were ridiculous. That world was now my home. Old

School Runescape (OSRS) is a game that involves spending your time to gain skill levels and get rewards for completing tasks. As you improve, you are rewarded with more interesting challenges, and access to more of the world. A wonderful metaphor for how I've always wanted life to be.

For a lot of people OSRS was a place to make friends, but this wasn't the case for me. I met a few people that I would talk to sometimes, but they never seemed real. I ended up playing the game on 'private'. I started watching YouTube videos and streamers, and I fell in love with the idea. I gave streaming a go, but in the end I wasn't really cut out for that either. I still play it because I love the game, but also because it helps to distract me from reality. When I played it every day, it was because I needed to be anywhere but here in the real world. Now that things are improving, I play it in much smaller amounts when I need some 'me' time.

Recently I went on a short trip to Cornwall with my boyfriend. My mental health wasn't in great shape in the weeks before the holiday, my anxiety and depression were in full force. So we went away for a week and it felt like the first time I was actually free. I left almost all of the bad vibes behind and really enjoyed myself. It gave my head some space to think. We mostly went hiking and I would take some pictures. During the night we would go to the beach and take pictures of the stars, and I finally found something I wanted to do.

When we returned home, I kept getting the urge to paint. I ignored it for a while because I've never been very good at art. But one day I gave in, bought some watercolours and started experimenting. I started an online drawing course that has no exams or deadlines. I started opening myself up to the creative side of things, the things that I had pushed away in the past because I would 'never get a proper job in those fields'. Now I've set up an Instagram account for my photography (@smortart if you're interested) and I'm starting to be more artistic. I'm even hoping to sell a selection of my own products in the future. This was something I had shown interest in as a child, but I was told that there was no point in trying since people wouldn't want to buy my postcards. If someone had supported my idea back then, perhaps I would have followed a completely different path.

But I've come to realise that whatever path you may be taking and whatever destination you see before you, there is no rush. The most important thing for me was to listen to myself and my needs. By understanding myself I discovered that I was bi-sexual. Thankfully this news didn't bother me, it was more like a 'well duh!' moment. After discovering this, it didn't feel like a big deal, so I didn't really have to come out to my friends. There was one point when a friend in college asked if I was straight. I just told her I was bi, and that was that. Then we moved onto a bigger moment for me. She asked if I had any other labels, since from some of the stories I'd told her, it seemed like I might be poly. I had no idea what she meant, so she described it as 'someone who has relationships with more than one person.' LIGHTBULB MOMENT. All of my childhood boyfriends suddenly made sense, but it meant I was in a bit of a situation. Since I acknowledged this part of me, I needed to make sure my needs were being met. But I had been in a monogamous relationship with my boyfriend for a long time, and I loved him. I knew the only way to feel better in myself was to explain to him how I felt. He had the option that day (and still does) to leave me, but I managed to assure him that loving other people doesn't make me love him any less.

Life is still tricky. I've applied for a few jobs, but ultimately my anxiety really damages my interview skills, and makes me feel like I wouldn't be good enough to work there anyway. Many employers put up advertisements for their vacancies, and say they are looking for 'an enthusiastic, hard-working team player or leader'. The pressure to be this person every day I work there is enough to give me a panic attack – even when I'm just thinking about handing in my CV. There's a vacancy in my local vets for a receptionist, which is something that would interest me. However, they are looking for someone who can *'deal with stressful situations',* apparently so does the local pet shop and card shop. This criteria is one that currently, I cannot meet.

I still need to find a way to financially sustain myself. I feel bad that my parents still give me pocket money and that's my only source of income. I'd love to be able to stick with something for long enough to actually see it work out, and start supporting myself. This book has given me some inspiration and motivation to spread my wings and explore my own paths. I've realised that following a career path isn't as important as everyone made it seem.

I still wouldn't mind having a career in the future, as long as it was something that I enjoyed. I'm still figuring out exactly what my passions are, but I know that I love chemistry (or at least the areas I understand), and I love psychology. I'm also lowkey interested in technology. The Facebook algorithms, the current rise of the abilities of AI and all the new and amazing gaming technology are all things I would be interested in looking into. But there's no rush and for now I'm concentrating on my mental wellbeing, and tending to my more creative side.

I'm going to be honest with you. We've had to skip over many important experiences and details that I would love to share, but I'll save them for my own story. This book has given me a great opportunity to reflect on my experiences and start piecing together the jigsaw of my life so far. I've been on a long journey trying to figure out who I am: what my morals are rather than what I've been taught. If anything in this section has inspired you to find yourself, or even if it's just made you feel as though mental health problems don't have to be the end, then I'm glad I could help.

There's one thing I'd like to suggest to everyone reading this. If you feel like you're in a confusing place or if you feel unhappy or incomplete, here's something you might like to try. It's something for everyone no matter your generational label or sexual identity. Whether you feel like you suffer from mental health problems or not, I ask you to look *after* yourselves by looking *at* yourself. I encourage you to write your own chapter. About your own life.

Looking back on my life, making sense of it and writing it all down has been amazingly therapeutic for me, and it's something I'd love for other people to experience too. But writing it down is only half the story. Sharing it with my family, friends and people that I trust has helped other people understand me better, and I don't feel like I'm carrying around secrets any more. If you do decide to share your story, feel free to let us see by tagging the post with #MyChapter.

4

Emerging Adults 80s Style

For Gen X and preceding generations, life was defined by three stages. You were a *child*, an *adolescent* or an *adult.* (There was also the *teenager*, but this was a sub-category that spanned child and adolescent.) In rare circumstances—such as going off to war—teenagers could find themselves thrust, ready or not, into early onset adulthood. Back then adults regularly referred to adolescents as *'a waste of space'*, usually preceded by any combination of disparaging adjectives selected randomly from a long and varied list. A list that included *disrespectful, lazy, ungrateful, expensive* and *tiresome.* In cases which justified multiple selections, it would be usual to condense them all into a single, heavily stressed word—*SPECTACULAR.* Any young person who drove an adult to refer to them as *'a SPECTACULAR waste of space'* had clearly mastered the art of adolescence. As you will no doubt have realised, this description of an adult's view of adolescents is fundamentally the same today as it was forty years ago.

Another similarity to today is that boundaries between the stages were roughly defined by age, with some uncertainty whether you became an adult at the age of 16 (see note on teenagers above), waited until you were 21, or somewhere in between the two. But, like it or not, you were ALWAYS considered an adult by the time you hit your 21st birthday, regardless of whether your behaviour and general maturity justified such a responsible title. Millennials claim they have invented a new life stage that formally delays the move into adulthood. It is known as an *emerging adult*, it appears to run into their early thirties, and is associated with another Millennial-inspired term, the *quarter life crisis*. If you have paid attention in earlier chapters of this book, you will know that I am well-positioned to offer expert insight into both phenomenon through Harriet, my emerging adult daughter who is experiencing her own full-on quarter life crisis.

I suppose the first thing I should mention is my belief that the quarter life crisis is a genuine Millennial invention. I certainly never flitted from job to job while agonising over whether I had made the right career choice, neither was I aware of anyone else whose career was delayed or disrupted by any such concern. It's quite possible there were a few free-spirited graduates out there who took a gap year to go trekking in the Himalayas, and ended up as Buddhist monks in a remote Tibetan monastery. But I never knew any—either personally or through the popular press. No. We all just got on with the business of earning a living throughout our 20s with the clear understanding that—should we need a crisis—the proper time to embark on that journey was in our late 40s when our own children had grown up. So, yes. I'm happy to award invention of the quarter life crisis to Millennials.

But Emerging Adults? Absolutely not. I can say with a high degree of confidence that this is not their invention. I accept that the term *Emerging Adult* was introduced to the world in 1994 by Jeffrey Jensen Arnett (a Baby Boomer and professor of psychology) with the purpose of being applied to Millennials. However, the behaviour he was describing wasn't significantly different from that of preceding generations. From my personal experience, I'd claim the main difference between Millennials and their parents is the backdrop against which this life stage is played out. Historically, the as-yet unnamed phase of personal growth, took place after you'd left home and had the security of employment. Even if parents knew of what was going on, they had no input. Today it's more likely young people will go through the same phase while living with their parents, and with at least some reliance on the Bank of Mum and Dad. For both generations the phase revolves around the same core concept of a desperate desire to avoid the reality that your youth is over, and it's time to move on to the overwhelming responsibilities of the next stage of your life.

A large chunk of my own emerging adulthood took place after I'd left university and had started work as an engineer at Rolls Royce. I met my future husband at a Bristol gathering of Rotoract, a club for young professionals based on the Rotary model used by serious grownups. It was a great place to meet new people, expand social life, try new activities and gain new life experiences. It was hardly love at first sight. After all, anyone with even a smattering of the French language would want to keep a safe distance from someone who was known by the name Mort. The first time he spoke to me was to tell me about the potholing trip that had been arranged for the coming weekend, and he asked me if I would like to sign up. Er, no thanks. I may be crazy, but spending hours underground in cold, wet caves with a guy who called himself by the French word for Death, did not appeal in the slightest. Another factor in turning down his kind offer was I was overweight, and the prospect of squeezing my size 14 body into a wetsuit horrified me. I enrolled for the cheese and wine trip instead.

Eventually I did get together with Mort—short for Mortimer—his surname. I think the turning point in our relationship was when he donated one of his old badminton racquets to me. A fancy racquet with a carbon fibre shaft to replace the archaic wooden one I had just broken was all it took. Suddenly I could hit a shuttlecock the whole length of the court, and I had Mort's cast-off racquet to thank.

Rotoract was brilliant. Weekends and evenings became a whirlwind of social activities, often revolving around food and alcohol, but always in a civilized—dare I say yuppie—way. Definition alert. The term *yuppie* was used in the 80s to describe young, upwardly mobile professionals. Maybe we should have been called *yumps*, but thankfully the person who invented the term called on a little artistic license. While doing research into the term I came across the following explanation of a yuppie on Wikipedia. It was written in 2016 by a guy called Paul Graham in an essay, claiming that the term arose because of changes in the nature of the job market at the start of the 1980s.[6] According to Wikipedia, Paul Graham is an English born computer scientist, entrepreneur, venture capitalist, author, and blogger. Here's what he wrote.

> By no coincidence it was in the early 1980s that the term "yuppie" was coined. That word is not much used now, because the phenomenon it describes is so taken for granted, but at the time it was a label for something novel. Yuppies were young professionals who made lots of money. To someone in their twenties today, this wouldn't seem worth naming. Why wouldn't young professionals make lots of money? But until the 1980s being underpaid early in your career was part of what it meant to be a professional. Young professionals were paying their dues, working their way up the ladder. The rewards would come later. What was novel about yuppies was that they wanted market price for the work they were doing now.

Wow. I had no idea I had been an active member of such a revolutionary movement. Kudos to me.

Within a couple of years Mort and I bought a house together, and as the purchase was going through, we went camping to the Isles of Scilly. I was quite happy slumming it in a tent as long as there was a reasonable expectation of at least some decent weather during the stay. Mort was a regular visitor to the location. He was full of stories about how beautiful the islands were, and all the things we could get up to during our idyllic fortnight away in glorious sunshine. I bought his story hook, line and sinker. As it turned out, this was

6 The Refragmentation http://paulgraham.com/re.html

one of many examples where plans did not turn out as expected as a direct result of my overly trusting nature. This, combined with a complete absence of the Internet to carry out even the most basic corroborating research. If I'd had prior knowledge of travel times from Bristol to Land's End in peak holiday season, and weather patterns off the coast of Cornwall in August, our plans may have been very different.

Our holiday got off to a bad start when—*at 3 o'clock in the morning*—we hit a jam-packed M5 just south of Bristol to join a million other travellers in nose-to-tail traffic that stretched 170 miles all the way to Penzance. So instead of our planned leisurely morning enjoying breakfast in a costal café, we spent 6 frustrating hours in increasingly desperate efforts to prevent the car engine going into a terminal state of meltdown. Once we'd arrived in Penzance, we had just enough time to attach ourselves to our heavily laden rucksacks, and sprint from the car park to the ferry terminal during the tropical storm which had been brewing (both metaphorically and literally) all morning. Then things went from bad to worse. A hideously rough journey on the Scillonian III Passenger Ferry from Penzance to Saint Mary's—the largest of the chain of 5 islands—was followed by another puke-inducing boat trip. This time our destination was Bryher, described in the Isles of Scilly Tourist Board's leaflet as 'a rugged yet deeply beautiful island of vibrant contrasts'. It may well have been endowed with all of these fine qualities, but the only thing I noticed was the non-stop torrential rain and high winds. As the first week drew to a soggy close, we awoke in the middle of the night with an urgent need to bail out our rapidly flooding tent. This was the final straw. With nowhere to dry our clothes or sleeping bags, I insisted on bringing the camping-trip-from-Hell to a premature end, and we packed up and departed for home.

Of course Misery wasn't ready to call it a day, it was having too much fun at our—no my—expense. As we sailed back home through raging seas Mort admitted it had been nearly as bad the last time he went, but he hadn't wanted to tell me the truth in case it had deterred me. This admission came so close to being a deal breaker in our relationship. I don't have the capacity for anger, but in between violent barfs, I'll admit that I directed a few well-chosen—and undeniably well-deserved—swear words at him. Thankfully this episode didn't derail our life together, and three decades later we are still happily married and living in the same house we bought shortly after returning from our memorable (for all the wrong reasons) holiday in the Isles of Scilly.

We bought the house, moved in together, and little changed for the next five years. Life still revolved around Rotoract and sports halls—I even became a reasonable club-standard badminton player, thanks largely to Mort's hand-me-down racquet. We shoehorned our wedding and honeymoon into our busy social lives. But after surviving an entire day wearing an assortment of dresses (unlike Cilla Black, I didn't feel comfortable turning up for my wedding in the Leeds United football strip), a mandatory visit inside a church for the wedding ceremony, eviction from our own wedding reception by the Liverpool Chapter of the Masonic Lodge, an awesome post-wedding Barn Dance, and finally a honeymoon staying in a proper hotel in the glorious sunshine of Minorca, life continued as before.

Although we were both working, we weren't rolling in money. For a house warming present my parents had generously bought us an expensive fitted carpet from John Lewis, which we installed throughout the hallway, stairs and landing. But apart from this luxury we got by with minimal furniture and basic cooking appliances that comprised a Baby Belling, an electric kettle and an ancient microwave oven. Not long after moving in we discovered a worrying problem in our loft that forced us to extend our mortgage so we could get urgent repairs done. It was that or risk the roof of our house collapsing into our bedroom at a very inconvenient moment.

We were regular victims of burglaries. Easy access to the back of the property, along with insecure wooden doors and windows, made us an attractive target for local scumbag thieves. In reality we had nothing worth stealing (apart from the carpet, but thankfully that was never targeted) but the thieves still took a load of second hand equipment we relied on, and they caused a lot of damage. They jimmied windows open destroying the frames and damaged the patio doors beyond repair. In one of several failed attempts they pulled a drainpipe down while trying to get into an upstairs bedroom. On another occasion I returned home to find a large hole had been carefully cut out of the back door, and our house was in a worse mess than we had left it when we had departed for work that morning. I can't be certain, but I suspect the hole in the door and the ransacked house were related. All of this caused us a lot of hassle filing police reports, completing insurance claims, and getting emergency repairs done. Still, being glass-half full people, we took each burglary as an opportunity to use the insurance pay-outs to partially fund a steady upgrade of our beloved home. We also took great pleasure when, during one incursion, the thieves left with a knackered TV that we were about to dispose of. Thanks scumbags, you saved us a journey to the council tip.

We were fortunate that our foray into home ownership coincided with Privatization—the Conservative Government's determined effort to sell off all the country's silverware at a bargain basement price. We were late to the game, having missed out on the first two phases which started as early as 1979. But by 1987—following their third consecutive election victory—the Tories were on a roll and we were champing at the bit, ready and eager to take advantage of the most aggressive stage of their privatisation programme. British Steel, British Petroleum, British Airways and Rolls Royce were all offered for sale, as were a number of major utilities, including water and electricity. With careful timing we could gamble the following month's mortgage payment on the latest share offer. We could do this with increasing confidence that not only would we get our money back in time to make the mortgage payment, we would also make a quick profit to pay for a new sofa, cooker or whatever was next on the shopping list.

A few months after our wedding, when I was approaching

the ripe old age of 27 and Mort had just moved into his 30s, I gradually became aware of a strange sensation. Maternal Instinct was kicking in accompanied by an uneasy sense that our lives had become shallow. We briefly discussed parenthood, but Mort reeled off a well-rehearsed and convincing list of reasons why he was still far too immature to become a father. I didn't fight it. How could I? He was clearly right, and my maternal instinct was still under-developed. So our shallow, hugely enjoyable, not-yet-proper-adult lives continued unchecked for another couple of years.

If I were to pick the single moment when we made the transition to proper adults, I would say it was during a conversation about an approaching skiing holiday, and the mortgage payment we would default on if we proceeded to pay the final instalment. It was this conversation that finally persuaded us of the need to take our financial responsibilities seriously. I guess I was 28, and Mort was in his early 30s.

Eventually the time was right to start a family, and we were pregnant. I hadn't realised that men could get pregnant, but it was a growing trend for couples to refer to pregnancy in this way, regardless of how little the male contributed over the nine-month gestation period. To be fair to David, who was now well into his thirties and showing increasing signs of maturity by dropping the name Mort, he embraced the whole preparing for parenthood thing. He declined offers of squash and badminton matches in favour of pre-natal classes and hospital visits for scans. He curtailed trips to the pub so he could use the newly purchased paint and wallpaper for their intended purpose (conversion of a drab bedroom into a welcoming, gender-neutral nursery). This was a great improvement on their previous role as dangerous obstacles for his heavily pregnant wife to navigate past on entering through the front door. But no sooner had he earned lots of brownie points for all the good things he'd done, than he spoiled it all by naming our developing foetus *Wazzock*. Why he chose this name is beyond me, but I happily embraced it having no idea that it wasn't a nice thing to call our unborn child. By the time I realized that it was a northern term often preceded by '*yah great, big, hairy*' it was too late, the name had stuck.

5

Motherhood

I would like to say I breezed through pregnancy in happy anticipation of the approaching birth of our first child. Maybe I did, but the reality is I remember very little about it. I suspect this is nature's defence mechanism kicking in to prevent me re-living the ordeal. I continued to work, and I recall doing stupid things like keying the 4-digit PIN for my bankcard into the coffee machine, then getting annoyed when instead of black coffee, it dispensed a luminous fizzy orange liquid that could easily have been nuclear waste. I'd understand if this had been a one-off. Isn't this something everyone does from time to time—pregnant or not? But on a daily basis? I can't believe that's normal. Not even for the exhausted, hormone-fuelled, nervous wreck of a human being I'd become. Mostly though, this period of my life is hidden beneath a thick, comforting blanket of fog under which I am reluctant to peek.

The process of giving birth terrified me. My pleas for a caesarean were rejected on the grounds that a natural birth would be a breeze as '*I had a birth canal the size of the Channel Tunnel*'. Well, let's just say on the day Wazzock entered the world the exit from the Channel Tunnel was blocked by a pile of rotting artichokes dumped by an army of angry French farmers. When Wazzock was handed over to me, the sheer enormity of my responsibility to this tiny, squealing alien hit home. Exhausted, overwhelmed and emotional, my first act of motherhood was to swear that Wazzock would be an only child.

I had no intention of EVER putting myself through that ordeal again.

Someone once asked me if I could be any animal, what would I choose. I surprised myself by replying without hesitation 'duck-billed platypus'. My conscious mind had never given this question any serious consideration—after all it was not like I would ever get the opportunity to change species. It wasn't even a subject I'd considered in the imaginary world of my childhood day dreams. I figured my subconscious had chosen this aquatic creature because it was quirky, it didn't fit in to any normal classification, and it spent its days swimming in the clear warm waters of Australia. An inspired choice. Now, having just been through the agony of human child birth, I realised there was another good reason to be a platypus—they are one of only a small group of mammals that reproduce by laying eggs. Females of the species lay a few eggs in a hole, then ten carefree days later the eggs hatch. If only human reproduction was that straight forward. My hopes that humans were heading in a similar direction had been raised when I first heard the term '*test-tube baby*'. What a fantastic idea. We fertilise one of my eggs in a Petri dish, then leave it to develop in a laboratory for 9 months while we get on with our stress-free lives. On our due date we rock up at the lab armed with a nappy, a baby-grow, a rear-facing car seat and a bunch of excited relatives. Then, having confirmed our identity, white-coated lab staff hand our new baby over to us and off we go—full steam ahead into parenthood. Once again my imagination was ahead of the game, and reality stretched no further than the part about the Petri dish.

Laying eggs isn't the only maternal pain-avoidance mechanism used in platypus reproduction. Get this. Female platypuses don't have nipples. Instead, when they nurse, milk oozes out of mammary gland ducts on their abdomen and babies drink by sucking it out of their mother's fur. Three weeks of mastitis and agonizing breasts could have been avoided if only evolution had been as kind to humans as it was to our distant mammalian cousins.

After the difficult start I took to motherhood like a duck-billed platypus to water, helped by the unyielding support of David, the now grown up husband and proud father. Maternity leave was the first real break I'd had since I'd left university nine years earlier, and I took every opportunity to join the endless round of coffee mornings. Anyone overhearing a coffee morning conversation between new mums would be forgiven for thinking they'd been transported to a strange universe. A place where adult women discuss the finer points of the contents of nappies, the best washing powders and how to remove vomit from a deep blue carpet.

Tiring of the social scene and the accompanying chocolate-fuelled weight gain, I had little hesitation returning to work when Harriet was just 3 months old. A new nursery had opened just a short walk away, and I was happy that this would be an ideal environment in which our tiny bundle of joy would thrive between 8am when we dropped her off, and 6pm when we turned up to reclaim her. She was well looked after and had an enviable life full of fun and games. I often picked her up long before closing time and witnessed her playing happily with the other children, or making all the right movements during reading time. In particular, she excelled (as did I) at the movements that accompanied Little Rabbit Foo Foo when he scooped up the wriggly worms and bopped them on their head.

Life was great. I was working mainly from home and I had surprisingly little to do, which gave me plenty of time to catch up on sleep and housework. The company I worked for was going through a major reorganisation and I have good reason to suspect they'd forgotten I was still on their list of employees. Not one to rock the boat, I kept quiet, made the occasional visit to the head office to show my face, and continued to pick up my monthly pay check. I knew this happy state of affairs wouldn't last forever. It continued for about twelve glorious months, by which time I was relaxed and happy in my life as a mummy, and had secured the job of my dreams in a well-known local Financial Services company. Within six months of starting the new job I was an exhausted wreck close to breaking point. Thankfully it was only a temporary setback, and it wasn't long until I had become a Zen Master in the art of work-life balance.

About that promise I made myself. You know, the one where I swore Wazzock would be an only child as I would never put myself through the misery of child birth again. Well, clearly I had been exhausted and extremely emotional at the time I made it. Surely child birth couldn't have been that bad could it? Even if it had been, we all survived and life was now peachy. Let's have another one. So after two miscarriages, and many cycles of hope followed by despair followed by more hope, along came our second daughter and our family was complete. (Apart from the array of animals that would join us at various points on our journey through life.) This time giving birth was a breeze, and a week before Christmas 1996 David whisked Harriet out of primary school to meet her newborn sister, Sally. Honestly, the 1989 film starring Billy Crystal and Meg Ryan had never crossed our mind when we picked the name Sally. Harriet had always been known either by her full name, or abbreviated simply to H. I'm not sure when the transformation occurred, but by the end of the first day of Sally's life, H had morphed into Harri, and Harri had well and truly met Sally.

A few months before my due date I was on a course at work that, owing to lack of space in the office, had been moved to a conference room at the local David Lloyd Tennis Centre. I arrived early and took the opportunity to look around before the first training session started. I had never seen an indoor tennis court before, and here was a place with dozens of them. There was also an indoor swimming pool where large, pregnant ladies were engaged in a surreal form of aquatic movement to music, a spectacle I later discovered was called *aquarobics*. There was also a sauna, squash courts, a well-stocked gym, an enviable list of after-school activities for children of all ages and, best of all, a crèche that took children from the age of zero up to eleven. They also ran school holiday clubs. I was hooked, and decided there and then that David Lloyd Centre would become my primary day time residence during my imminent four month maternity break. David, being a racquet-sporty person was all for it. The prospect of being able to play tennis, badminton and squash all on the same day and under the same roof was nothing short of a dream come true.

We signed up for family membership. After Sally was born I established a well-drilled routine that involved dropping Harriet off at primary school, then heading straight to the club to use the gym. I'd then be free to play tennis or relax in the spa pool, with Sally either secured nearby in her portable car seat or in the on-site crèche. A few times a week I even took Sally with me to the post-natal aquarobics class for new mums and their babies. In the afternoon I'd have lunch and relax in the comfortable lounge before setting off to pick Harriet up from school. Most evenings we'd go straight back to David Lloyd Centre for the after-school swimming and ballet classes for which I had enrolled Harriet. I had been an excellent swimmer before puberty kicked in, and it was clearly important that children learned to swim, but why I signed her up for ballet class remains a mystery. My younger sister—the normal, inoffensive sibling I barely remember until I hit my late teens—spent many years attending the Vernon Johnson School of Ballet in Liverpool, and I occasionally tagged along to watch. At the time I thought it was hilarious, nevertheless it seemed a necessary skill for my own daughter to master. I dutifully purchased the long list of essential clothing required for a budding ballerina.

Getting a five-year-old dressed for a ballet lesson was a new experience for me. It took a full fifteen minutes to get her out of her school uniform and into the new pastel blue ballet outfit. Tights before leotard, then tutu, then wrap-around cardigan and ballet shoes. When all this was finished, work some magic on her hair so it doesn't flop in her face and distract her from her pirouettes and pas de deux. All done, we make the short journey from changing room to the dance studio with a few minutes to spare. 'Mummy', she says in a quiet and embarrassed voice, 'I need to go for a wee.' Back down to the changing room, remove wrap-around cardigan and tutu, pull down leotard, tights and pants. Wee. Put everything back on, making sure it's done in the right order. Then return to the dance studio just as twenty tiny girls are doing their best impersonations of a tree blowing in the wind. 'Mummy, why are they all waving their arms like that and falling over like they're broken?' she asks. 'I have absolutely no idea my sweet, maybe if you join in, you'll find out'. So off she toddled and pretended to be a tree. Ah, bless.

DLC (as David Lloyd Centre will be referred to from this point forward) became home from home, and we would spend most of our evenings and weekends there. We'd have dinner there, Harriet would do her homework there, and she started tennis coaching as well as swimming. Sadly ballet didn't last long. After several weeks of the same maddening routine of getting her kitted up before she decided she needed a wee, I realised this was her endearing, childlike way of telling me she hated it. Please, please, please don't make me go again. If she had just come out and said 'mummy I hate this, make it stop', I would have withdrawn her at once. It seems my ability to pick up on subtle messages was just as underdeveloped for my own daughters as it was for humanity in general.

In an ideal world DLC would have offered us a furnished on-site apartment (with a washing machine and built-in dryer) to save us the hassle of going home every night. But as this wasn't on the list of membership options, we reluctantly packed up each evening for the twenty minute drive home. We'd then navigate two exhausted girls past the growing pile of smelly towels and sweaty sports kit that littered the hallway, read them a story and get them off to bed.

Story time for Harriet brought the adventures of another Harry into our lives. J. K. Rowling had just released The Philosopher's Stone, the first of the Harry Potter series. What a brilliant story it was. Wizards and muggles, magical trains accessible by walking through a wall at Kings Cross Station. Pet owls and toads, vomit-flavoured jelly beans, Norbert the Norwegian Ridgeback dragon… I was completely hooked. The staple diet of my childhood reading had been Enid Blyton's Famous Five and Secret Seven. Like many other young children at the time, I had enjoyed the exciting adventures that revolved around a group of young detectives and their dog. Adventures that had one thing in common—no self-respecting child would be seen dead reading them after the age of ten. This sudden loss of interest was not because we feared endless ridicule from our class mates, but simply because the stories were incredibly lame and predictable. The Harry Potter series was entirely different and was devoured by adults and children alike. Regardless of your age, there was no shame in being seen on a bus or walking down the road or even sitting at your desk (office or classroom) feeding your addiction. My interest eventually drifted away, but Harry Potter became such an important part of Harriet's life that even as she approaches her 26th birthday she can often be seen reading from her cherished collection of hardback books, or watching one of the films for the gazillionth time.

Back in the far less interesting muggle world, our involvement with DLC got us well and truly caught up in the ultra-competitive junior tennis scene. Before we knew it our lives revolved around where Harriet's next ranking points were coming from. Competitive match followed competitive match. Every month we eagerly poured over the updated rankings and local leagues to assess who had moved up, and who to play in the next monthly session to maximise the opportunity of winning precious ranking points. Harriet's tennis training moved to a whole new level when, twice a week, we left home for DLC at 7 in the morning so she could take part in an hour of drills before whisking her to primary school in time for the 8.50 start. The whole setup was beyond crazy. She was barely ten years old.

One day Harriet complained about a persistent pain in both her lower legs so we took her to the doctors. We guessed she had shin splints, a problem that many of the child tennis players suffered as their growing bodies were pushed well beyond healthy limits. The GP confirmed this and added reassuringly 'She'll need to rest for a few weeks, and she'll be fine.' My vocal chords disengaged from my brain to deliver a calm response of 'OK, that makes sense, we'll keep her away from training'. At the same time my brain was desperately trying to express my actual feelings that was something along the lines of 'you must be f*****g insane!!! She's got four massively important tennis matches lined up. If she doesn't play them, she definitely won't move up a league, and she may even drop down one!!!. That can't be allowed to happen. What pain relief can you give her so she can continue to play?' Fortunately something deep inside me knew a rant of this nature would have triggered a visit from the Child Protection Services and my daughter would have been instantly removed from her very, very bad mother.

This was a wakeup call, and I became much more aware of the damage excessive training was doing to her physical health. We cut back on tennis coaching and competitive matches and picked up badminton instead. One of the badminton coaches at DLC had spotted Harriet practicing with David, and suggested she came along to the county selection day that was a few weeks away. That was the start of her rise through junior badminton. Within a few weeks she'd progressed from a complete beginner to being a sought after member of Avon county squad. With girls in short supply she regularly found herself playing—and winning—against much older players. While the tennis setup had been all about the individual and obscenely competitive, badminton was much more team-focused, relaxed and enjoyable. The main downside with badminton was the travel involved. Tennis had always been local, and only rarely had we travelled more than half an hour to get to a venue. As we were about to find out, badminton was an entirely different world that would involve becoming familiar with the geography of England, the motorway network and the inside of Travelodge bedrooms.

The last year at primary school was busy for Harriet. Not only did she have tennis and badminton to keep her busy, we were also preparing her for an entrance exam into an independent school. Preparation involved endless hours working through hundreds of verbal reasoning questions from sample exam papers, writing essays and preparing for interviews. This was undoubtedly more unnecessary stress in her life, as she would probably have sailed through the exams with only a fraction of the effort. But getting into a school that was right for her was too important to take unnecessary risks.

We decided to send our girls to independent secondary schools when Harriet still had several years left at her state primary school. The decision was not taken lightly as we knew it would be a massive financial commitment. The problem we faced was that secondary education in the area of Bristol where we lived seemed to be little short of a complete disaster. Most of the good schools had abandoned the state sector and set up independently. Of those that remained, either they didn't have a 6th form—which we considered essential—or they were heavily oversubscribed, and too far away for us to stand any chance of the girls getting a place. We considered moving into the catchment area of a good school, but this would have meant either dramatically increasing our mortgage or moving to a much smaller house with a much smaller garden, neither of which we were willing to do. Even if we had moved, there was no guarantee the catchment area wouldn't shrink further as desperate parents were paying well over the odds for properties closer and closer to the good schools. We also felt that just because a school was good at one point in time, it didn't necessarily mean it would stay that way. We had come across several examples where the change of head teacher led to significant degradation in the quality of the school.

As the girls grew up, it became increasingly difficult to juggle our full-time jobs with the inconvenience of a 3.15pm kick out from school, and every school holiday that lasted for more than a week was a complete organisational nightmare. After months of struggle, we came to the conclusion that one of us would have to give up work. We selected who would take on full-time parental responsibility by scoring ourselves against a short, weighted list of things that were important to us. I don't remember what was on it except for two high valued items: medium-term earning potential and enjoyment of work. I won the right to continue in employment by a country mile. While David joined the emerging ranks of New Age Men and became a househusband.

6

Confronting the Mental Health Monster

Before getting stuck into this chapter, I will tell you a story about the worst four weeks of my life. Not the full, deeply disturbing details, as those are still locked away in a dark recess of my mind guarded by a solid door bearing a sign 'Gateway to Hell. Do Not Enter'. But enough to give you a flavour of what people were willing to put themselves through to find success in the inhospitable workplaces of the mid to late 1980s. Workplaces in which untrained managers experimented with their own pet theories on how to get the best out of their employees. Workplaces in which no one above the lowest pay grade gave a shit about mental health. European Union regulations limiting working hours were still several years away. As was any concept of employees being entitled to a reasonable work-life balance. It was simple back then. If you wanted a good job that paid well, suck it up, and don't go crying if things get tough. Booh hoo hoo. Nobody cares. If you can't hack it, fuck off you're no use, you're replaceable. Go get yourself a job at Woolworths.

Throughout my early years at work there was a real focus on understanding your personal strengths and weaknesses, self-improvement and getting out of your comfort zone. Back in those days my comfort zone didn't stretch much beyond the imaginary wall that surrounded my desk and keyboard. But success at work demanded that I knocked down sections of the wall and let in messy people skills, before reconstructing the wall a little further out. Recover for a few weeks, take stock, then go through the whole unedifying process again.

I hated giving presentations, particularly if I didn't have a solid grasp of the subject. I also hated being in big groups, but the thing I hated most of all was making small talk with people I didn't know. (Apparently confident professionals had their own word for this small talk—they called it *'networking'*.) So when my boss told me I was to attend an engineering conference at the University of Nottingham, where I would give a presentation on Modal Analysis in an auditorium full of engineering students, professors and industry leaders, it's fair to say the prospect filled me with horror. Then—as if that was not enough torment for one day—I would introduce myself to senior decision makers over lunch. By the end of the day I would leave the event with an extensive network of contacts to help bring in future work. INTRODUCE MYSELF TO COMPLETE STRANGERS—I couldn't imagine anything worse. No wait, I could. There was something far worse than that: Introduce myself to complete strangers who also happened to be *successful business leaders*. My prior state of horror instantly transitioned into unimaginable dread. I wanted the ground to open up and swallow me. Actually, this was my second choice of outcome. First choice was for the ground to open up and suck the life out of my boss, while he writhed around in agony, slowly dissolving in his own stomach acid. I wouldn't normally have considered such an extreme form of torture for my boss—he was one of the good guys—but my reaction was a reflection of the level of terror which now engulfed me. Oblivious to my state, he rattled on about how it would take me out of my comfort zone and would be *'character building'*. It nearly destroyed me. Sure, Modal Analysis wasn't a complete mystery to me—I had a dry text book and had been working on a related computer program for all of two months. That hardly made me an expert, certainly nowhere near as knowledgeable as many of the attendees of the conference.

The only way of getting out of this date with destiny was to leave, or die. Saying 'I'm sorry but I'm not ready to do this' wasn't acceptable back then, and I had just found out I was in the early stages of my first pregnancy, so leaving my job wasn't a realistic option and neither was dying. I just had to push through for the next four weeks until the ordeal was over. The effort and stress would surely be well-rewarded by the magical new skills I'd gain, and I'd forever be an expert in giving sparkling presentations on subjects I knew or cared little about. I spent every waking hour outside of work (apparently character building was only effective if you did it in your own time) writing my half-hour talk and learning it verbatim. Reading from a script, I was informed, didn't build character in the same way as presenting from memory in a natural, conversational style. And we were still in the 80s. This was long before PowerPoint entered the world to make presentations more visually appealing, while at the same time providing useful prompts for the novice speaker.

Two weeks into this first of several return trips to Hell, I had made progress with the presentation, but my stress levels where steadily increasing as the dreaded day approached. I miscarried at 10 weeks, spent the day in tears before dragging myself back to work to get on with my job (which I enjoyed) and the presentation (which I hated with every ounce of my being). Did the stress cause the miscarriage? Maybe, maybe not. Apparently miscarriage is quite a normal outcome of many first pregnancies. The day of the presentation came. It was such an awful experience that I immediately suppressed the details and have no wish to revisit them. Did the experience give me any of the promised benefits? Absolutely not. It led me to reinforcing the walls around my comfort zone, making them thicker and higher, building a solid, impenetrable roof over the top and filling in any tiny gap through which false promises of 'people skills' might creep in unnoticed. I decorated the inside of my sanctuary with a calming blue sky, bright sunshine, fluffy white clouds and pretty flowers. On the outside, I displayed a large sign that said *'If your question isn't about programming or engineering, kindly FUCK OFF I'm not interested'*. (I had learned the joys of swearing while working on the shop floor at Rolls Royce. And, while not yet ready to abandon my polite convent school upbringing, I was tentatively introducing the occasional curse into the language of my imaginary world. It was several years before I felt ready to change the sign to something less confrontational and start the slow process of dismantling the protective barrier.)

I have shared this story because it provides added insight into the foundations of my ingrained belief that mental health issues were largely a by-product of a self-indulgent, entitled generation prone to excessive navel-gazing. Apart from general quirkiness and regular outbreaks of sibling warfare, I'd had a fairly normal upbringing in a stable, loving family. I certainly hadn't been mentally toughened up by spending any time at the school of hard knocks. Yet I had been through all this workplace shit and found a way to cope. I had never once considered myself to be depressed—most definitely stressed, annoyed, physically and mentally exhausted, even profoundly unhappy—but never depressed. Not once did I have an overwhelming urge to run off to the Ladies and sob my heart out; or take an unofficial '*duvet day*'; or visit my GP and ask for pills and be signed off work with stress. These things never crossed my mind. I simply accepted the experience as a necessary evil and got on with it.

My earlier views on mental health were dramatically and painfully demolished one day in July 2013. It started off a beautiful day. We were on a boat trip half way through a family holiday in the eastern Mediterranean, with the wind in our hair, the sun shining and surrounded by other happy holiday makers. I didn't have a care in the world. Sally was out on deck staring into the distance. Strangely for someone desperate to get a suntan, she was wearing a loose white cardigan on top of her bikini. Assuming it was to prevent her getting burnt, I offered her suntan cream which she declined. The boat dropped anchor and we all happily launched ourselves over the side to swim and snorkel in the enticing, clear blue sea. We larked about in the water, swam to the nearby beach and larked about some more. Life really didn't get much better than this. When the time came for the boat to continue its leisurely journey around the Greek Islands, I got back on board, closely followed by Sally. She walked over to the bench where she had left her cardigan, and as she reached over to pick it up, that's when I saw the scars; dozens of ugly, angry, snarling red lines criss-crossing her lower left arm, disappearing below the array of colourful bands and bracelets she always wore around her wrist. She noticed me staring, and that was it. She knew her dark, desperate secret was out. She didn't attempt to put the cardigan back on, instead we fell into each other's arms, held on tight and cried; intense, heart-wrenching tears the like of which I had never experienced before. I don't know how long we held each other like this, but I do know I never wanted to release her from my protective maternal embrace. I would have done anything to free her from her terrible pain; to suck out every single drop of her misery and take it all for myself. Unlike my beautiful, quirky, sensitive daughter I was tough, I could handle it. But that's not the way these things work, and life can be incredibly cruel and unforgiving. I have never felt as inadequate and utterly helpless as I did on that day in July 2013 when I finally realised that Sally had a mental illness.

There had been signs she was unhappy. She was often extremely reluctant to get out of bed in the morning. Sometimes in the car on the way into school she became tearful and, claiming exhaustion after a bad night's sleep, begged me to take her home. I usually obliged, but it was a struggle to supress my frustration—taking her home inevitably led to a much longer journey into work as I got caught up in Bristol's notorious rush-hour traffic. Then there were occasions when I'd pick her up from friends' birthday parties to find out she'd spent the entire evening in tears after someone had 'been mean to her'. I put all of this down to normal teenage angst, and it was just a phase in her life that would pass. She would, I was certain, come out the other end as tough and unconcerned about what others thought as I was—after all her DNA seemed pretty much identical to my own. I had never once considered these problems to be signs of a mental illness. Bi-polar and Schizophrenia—they're mental illnesses. I'd even learnt to accept anorexia and bulimia in that category. But unhappiness and stress brought on by our nation's tough examination system, the normal bitchiness of teenage girls, and life in general? No way did I consider these to be signs of mental illness. She did however have a nagging physical health problem that manifested itself as dizzy spells, which she described as feeling as though she was on the deck of a ship in rough water, or that the world was spinning around her. I took this seriously and accompanied her on many visits to her GP and paediatric specialists. She was subjected to a battery of tests, but no cause was ever identified and she was eventually discharged without ever getting a satisfactory diagnosis.

Now, faced with the physical evidence of self-harm, I was about to become intimately familiar with the mental health services on offer through the NHS, and it would forever change my views about mental illness.

I'm not sure what I expected when I accompanied her to see her GP on our return from holiday. I guess I was hoping she would get access to counselling which would magically get to the root of her problems, she'd be cured and life would go on as normal. As I've said before, I'm one of life's optimists. Her GP was very understanding, and the clear evidence of self-harm pushed her high up the list for referral to the Child and Adolescent Mental Health Service, CAMHS. On her first visit her appointment followed directly after a girl who had been in the same class at primary school. I later found out that at least one other pupil from that class of about thirty also has mental health problems. That's at least ten percent of her class. Frightening.

She was referred to CAMHS shortly after starting 6th form, having just achieved an amazing set of GCSE results that put her in the top few percent in the country. Results that were even more stunning given they were achieved against a backdrop of self-harm and abject misery. Her exam success had put her on a temporary high, and she was not ready to let anyone at school know about her mental health problems, or that she was seeing a psychiatrist.

So for the fortnightly CAMHS appointments which followed, she would take time off school for unspecified hospital appointments. She was also taking a lot of time off through exhaustion and normal physical ailments. Her work was suffering, and eventually we let the school know the truth behind her poor attendance and grades. We arranged a meeting with her teachers, and we all agreed the best thing to do was reduce the number of A-levels she was studying from four down to two. We knew this would not be enough to get her a place at university, but she was adamant she didn't want to go.

Sally struggled on through school and medical appointments. She was prescribed anti-depressants and anti-anxiety medication that would often put her into a deep sleep. On many occasions she fell into an almost comatose state where she would remain for an entire day. When she finally woke up, she was still exhausted and barely able to function. But at least she woke up. I can't find words to describe the utter terror I endured when approaching her lifeless body, or the tsunami of relief that swept over me when I reached out and felt the warmth of her skin. Another side effect of the medication was it destroyed her ability to concentrate. It was heart breaking to witness her rapid decline from a bright, able student, to someone who could barely do the most straightforward subtraction.

Sally continued through the first year of 6th form and sat a few exams with no realistic prospect of getting good grades. Then, while she was away volunteering on a conservation programme in Botswana, I got confirmation that her grades weren't good enough to move into the second year of 6th form. Her poor results were a relief as it took the decision out of our hands. Although the school would have taken her back to re-sit the year, we knew deep down that she needed to be removed from the education system to allow her to focus all her energies on getting better. So, while Sally was 5,600 miles away from me in Africa, I came to terms with the devastating reality she was dropping out of school, and that she wouldn't be completing A-levels then going on to university. Instead she was about to engage in a full-time battle to tame her own personal mental health monster. With her future now unclear, my optimism took temporary leave of absence.

Four years later, as her old school friends prepare to sit their final exams in university halls up and down the country, Sally's battle continues. Her 18th birthday marked a difficult milestone. No longer classified as an adolescent in the eyes of the NHS, her appointments with the psychiatrists at CAMHS stopped, and no equivalent service was offered. She enrolled onto a number of local programmes and self-help groups, which provided a degree of continuity and relief. Off-the-Record, and the perfectly named Happiness Project were two of the stand-outs. Her GP was amazing until he upped sticks and went to live in New Zealand, bringing more disruption to her already broken, directionless life. After a year of painfully slow progress, and when Sally was at a desperately low point, she started private counselling. She gradually came off her medication, and slowly but surely the weekly sessions had a positive impact on her life. She began to gain an understanding of the main triggers for her anxiety and depression, and to develop many techniques to protect herself against them. Probably the most profound impact was the discovery of the term '*empath*' and the realisation that it was a near-perfect match to the way she had felt throughout her life, from her earliest memories. It has proved to be a stunning discovery—one that goes a long way to explaining the reasons she developed mental illness. Most importantly, it gave us all real hope for her future. It is such an important subject that I have set aside an entire chapter to explore it.

Whilst Sally has been engaged in her highly visible struggles, Harriet has had her own challenges. It wouldn't be unreasonable to put Harriet in the category of someone who has it all in life. She is beautiful, confident, well-travelled, enjoys the companionship of a wonderful collection of close friends. She has achieved amazing academic and sporting success and, such was the respect from her peers and teachers, she was appointed to the prestigious position of Senior Prefect in her final year of 6th form. Her hard work at school and then university has been well-rewarded by excellent exam results, followed by an honours degree in Psychology and fantastic employment opportunities.

Of course life hasn't always been plain sailing for Harriet, and there have been hiccups along the way. Long before Sally's problems became evident, Harriet told me she felt a dark, immovable cloud surrounding her, a cloud she called depression. We paid a visit to her GP who pointed her toward local support groups and online resources. As far as I was concerned that was it. Problem sorted. We didn't really talk about her issues or concerns. In my view her life was perfect, and she was just going through a normal period of teenage angst. In the car journeys home from school I'd try to engage her in conversation—I'd ask her how her day had been, or what her plans were for the evening. Occasionally she rewarded my efforts at communication with an 'OK' or 'homework', but more often than not any audible response would most accurately be described as a grunt. In my own teenage years I treated my parents to similar displays of communication that even our Neanderthal cousins would have considered basic. It was perfectly normal teenage behaviour. Just a hiccup. Nothing to worry about. Even now, with the benefit of hindsight, I stand by this. Her periods of unwelcome grumpiness were transient and seemed to result from proximity to myself or David. In the company of her friends or her teachers, she always seemed to be her normal assured, confident and happy self.

The only time Harriet's health gave me real cause for concern was during her first year at university when she was constantly exhausted. She underwent a battery of tests for ailments commonly suffered by students in their fresher year—including glandular fever. They all came back negative. We shared plenty of phone calls throughout this period during which she would burst into tears, but by the end of the call she would always be calm and reasonably positive. It was her own steely determination, along with the support of her friends and tutors, which gave her the will-power to pull herself out of bed most days and get to the university gym, where gentle exercise eventually helped her back to health.

I have no wish to trivialise the health problems Harriet has faced throughout her life as they have undoubtedly been real and caused her considerable distress. However, the obstacles that have blocked her path have always seemed moveable with rest, tweaks in lifestyle, a night out with her friends or a good cry.

7

An Empath in the Family

I had never come across the word *'empath'* until Sally told me she is one. It's the label used by people who occupy the opposite end of the scale to where many narcissists and empathy-starved sociopaths hang out. She explained how she soaks up the emotions of others and literally feels their suffering or happiness. So not only does she have her own mixed up emotions to deal with, she accumulates the negativity from the world around her. All too often this leaves her an exhausted and emotional train wreck.

Prior to Sally's mental health problems, I would have considered this to be more self-indulgent nonsense. The old me would have summoned up the most comforting maternal tone I could manage to reassure her it was just a passing phase she would grow out of. While the voice in my head would be screaming *'For god's sake get a grip won't you. Life can be shit. Deal with it'*. It's fair to say the old me was paddling in the shallow end of the empathy pool.

Over the last 5 years I have learned to accept the reality of Sally's mental health problems. I know she hates being the way she is, and if she could 'get a grip' she would have done so a long time ago. She spends a lot of time researching mental health issues and trying to find coping strategies that work for her. I was certain she didn't label herself an empath on a whim, so I turned to Google for more information. 'What is an empath?' I ask. To which Google helpfully replies with a list of over half a million hits. The consensus of the dozen sites I investigate is similar to Sally's description—someone who absorbs the emotions of others into their own body and mind. There are numerous quizzes and checklists to help you identify if you are one, and it's clear there is a significant community of people who associate themselves with the term. Many of the links lead to Dr Judith Orloff who, according to her own website[7] is 'a psychiatrist, an empath and intuitive healer, and is on the UCLA Psychiatric Clinical Faculty.' She's a medical doctor, trained psychiatrist and respected public speaker, so I felt confident in selecting her as my authoritative source of further information. I purchased two copies of her book *The Empath's Survival Guide*, completed the 20-question quiz and, with a score of 5, confirmed that I'm at the low end of the empathy spectrum. Sally scored 18. Full-on empath.

Want to find out if you're an Empath? Try Dr Orloff's quiz.

If the old me had flicked through *The Empath's Survival Guide,* I would quickly have placed it in the same category as astrology, crystal healing and ley lines—all of which I readily dismiss as pseudoscientific mumbo jumbo. I would have shook my head in complete disbelief as I opened the book on the page which defined a number of general types of empaths, and read *'Plant Empaths can feel the needs of plants and connect with their essence'*, or *'Mediumship Empaths can access spirts on the Other Side.'* Or on another page, found the advice that parents of empaths should give their sensitive child *'a quartz or pink or black tourmaline crystal to hold'*. SERIOUSLY.

7 https://drjudithorloff.com

Do people actually believe this nonsense? If I'd then gone on to notice that the book was written by a medical doctor, I would have been shocked—or even horrified. How could a 'proper' doctor be peddling such complete and utter unscientific claptrap?

When Sally told me there was so much in the book that resonates with the way she feels—and has always felt—I was prepared to dump my deep-rooted scepticism, take a leap of faith, and approach the subject with an open mind. Now, having read the book, I'll admit to being amazed at how much made sense on an intellectual level, even though I don't 'get it' on a physical level. Personally I don't tend to get angry or distressed. It doesn't matter how hard I try I cannot sense *'toxic energy'*. I have no problem being crammed in a rush hour train on the London Underground, neither have I ever experienced *'bad energy'* left by an earlier occupant of my hotel room. None of this has ever caused me a problem, so I have never needed to learn techniques to deal with it. But *The Empath's Survival Guide* isn't about teaching empathically challenged people like myself to become more sensitive. The primary purpose of the book is to help empaths such as Sally learn how to tame the demon, convert it from a devastating curse into a manageable condition, and then—the ultimate goal—into an awesome gift. Although I don't 'get it', I have made the choice to believe every word—because it gives me grounds for real optimism about Sally's future. If she can master even a few of the techniques taught in the book, she can look forward to a happy, productive and medication-free life. And that is a hugely exciting prospect.

Although I'm unable to engage on an emotional level and truly understand how Sally experiences the world around her, *The Empath's Survival Guide* has given me a tremendous insight into her condition. The book refers to fascinating scientific studies that are throwing light on the neurological basis for empathy. One which I found particularly interesting was something called *mirror-touch synesthesia*, a rare condition in which people experience the same tactile sensation that another person feels. For example, if a person with the condition observes someone being touched on the cheek, they will experience the same sensation in their own cheek. Mirror-touch is just one of many forms of synesthesia, which is a well-documented condition in which two or more senses overlap. In other forms people can taste a particular word, perhaps October has the taste of a strong cheese; while others with the condition can smell a colour. It's a subject that has fascinated me since I first came across the condition in *Musicophilia*, a book by eminent neurologist Dr Oliver Sacks—one of my long-time favourite authors. In the book he describes several cases of musicians who attach a colour to a particular piece of music. Franz Liszt for example, was reported to demand his orchestra to 'play a little bluer' or appeal for 'more red!' Not surprisingly, his fellow musicians had no idea what he meant, and I suspect many of them thought he was nuts. Other famous synesthetes include Marilyn Monroe, Mary J. Blige and Richard Feynman, winner of the 1965 Nobel Prize in Physics. Among the less famous people with the condition is my elder daughter Harriet—in her case every number and letter has its own distinct colour. This is one of the more common forms, and is known as *grapheme-colour synesthesia*.

Since I discovered this anomaly in my first-born child, she has regaled me with fascinating insights into her multi-coloured world of words. For example, she has just told me that she will never change her surname because she loves the 'rouge-ness of it'. I've heard many reasons why married women keep their maiden names, but I can honestly say its colour was not one of them. In the very next sentence she added that she has never liked the name Hattie because 'the two dark blue letter *t*s ruin the overall redness'. This shocking news was followed by the revelation that 'Haz'—which she is called by many of her friends—'is OK because the end z is greyish and doesn't detract from the predominant red'. Worried that I might be calling her by a name that causes her immense visual distress, I nervously asked her what she thought of 'Harri'. It was a relief to find this was OK, although she admitted the final yellow 'i' can be a bit of a distraction. Enough strangeness, I think I need to take a nap.

Back to Dr Orloff's book and, as I mentioned before the diversion through the colours of Harriet's mind, the intriguing scientific explanations of empathy and empaths that are emerging from the world of academia. The primary theory of mirror-touch synaesthesia is based on the actions of mirror neurons. These were first observed in primates towards the end of the last millennium when a bunch of Italian researchers at the University of Parma inserted electrodes into the brains of macaque monkeys. I'm not going to debate the rights or wrongs of this, nor am I going to quote a bunch of academic studies that have been carried out in the field. Instead I will enlighten you with a wholly non-scientific—and possibly wildly inaccurate—interpretation of what I've read. (Hey, give me a break. I'm no neuroscientist, and there are many contradictory academic papers out there all of which contain long, complicated explanations. Worse still, they're overflowing with language that my lack of attention in Latin lessons has left me woefully unable to get to grips with.) These concerns aside, my summary should be easy for anyone with even the slightest whiff of empathy to understand. You'll get maximum insight if you try to visualise the example rather than just reading it. Here goes...

If you watch someone getting hurt—for the sake of dramatic effect, let's say a nasty, leg-breaking tackle in a game of football, or a knock-out punch in the boxing ring—the tendency is to recoil, make a contorted facial expression and utter a monosyllabic exclamation such as *uggh*, *yuck*, *ooooooh* or even the more extravagant *fuuuuuuuuuck*. This simple reflex action involves multiple regions of the brain, and is a normal human response. Mirror-touch synesthetes experience the same response, but with the important difference that their mirror neurons go into overdrive and activate the same *pain* pathways that would have been triggered if they'd suffered the actual tackle or punch themselves. So that's mirror-touch synaesthesia in a nutshell. I suspect most people with this condition don't have *Match of the Day* high up their list of favourite TV shows. Neither will they thank me for my earlier suggestion they visualise the example.

Sorry, how thoughtless of me. Moving on. Some researchers believe empathy has a similar mechanism, but deals with emotions rather than physical touch. The long and short of this condition is that when someone with a normal level of empathy witnesses a person in emotional distress, they will be sad for that person. However if an empath witnesses the same distress, not only will they feel sad for the person, but their mirror neurons will also trick their brain into activating the other person's emotions in their own neural pathways. Although this is true of both positive and negative emotions, it's not a case they balance each other out. Until empaths learn to be selective, the onslaught of emotions can leave them exhausted.

The Internet is awash with information relating to all forms of synesthesia. As I dug further into the mirror-touch form, I came across Dr Joel Salinas, a doctor of neurology at Harvard, who has the condition himself. Dr Salinas can literally feel the pain of his patients. This information has left me in no doubt that synesthesia is unquestionably real and comes in many varieties. Harriet's condition has had no negative impact on her life, while it seems possible—even probable—that Sally's unconventional brain wiring has been a major contributory factor in her mental illness.

I've always been taught you should face your fears. If you're terrified of flying, book yourself and a therapist or trusted friend on a cheap flight and go for it. When nothing bad happens, do it again. And again. Reward your efforts, perhaps with a night in a nice hotel in any distant destination that takes your fancy. If you're terrified of spiders, seek out a spider-infested basement and spend the night there in perfect darkness—alone. Ugghh, maybe that's extreme—it creeps me out just writing the words. But you get what I mean? The message I grew up with was to immerse yourself in your fears, and over time you will become desensitised. Of course, there were many far less welcome outcomes which didn't tend to get publicised. For example, you might die of a terror-induced heart attack, but either way your fears are gone. At the start of the last chapter I explained how I had been a reluctant participant in this approach myself. Sure, I did eventually get over my fear of giving presentations—but not until I'd been through a long, drawn out period in hell. In my case, I'm sure there were much better ways of dealing with my fear, and the ends definitely did not justify the means. Start small and gradually build up may well have been a much more effective and less disturbing route to success.

In her book, Dr Orloff suggests that the advice to 'face your fears' is inappropriate if you're an empath—or indeed if you are prone to any stress-related condition. Instead, she makes the simple recommendation that if you know something will make you unhappy—avoid it. For example, if you know driving at high speed on a motorway scares you shitless, take the side roads instead. Sure, it might take you longer to reach your destination, so leave yourself extra time. I suppose it's obvious, really. Sally recently tried this technique with great success to overcome a problem that was preventing her from playing her beloved Runescape, an online game that has proved to be an effective replacement for her anti-depression medication. In order to progress she had to complete a wacky quest which was proving too difficult. The quest took roughly fifteen minutes to complete, but whenever she failed, she'd have to start again—even when she got within a single mouse-click of success. After the first few failures, she was getting increasingly depressed—to the point where she stopped playing for several weeks. This was a big deal for her. She desperately wanted to get back to the game, but this massive brick wall was preventing her. One day she sat down with her boyfriend (who was able to stay calm and focused) and he suggested she spent the afternoon attempting the quest for as long as it took for her to complete it, then they'd go out and celebrate with a pizza. Sally, calling on the advice she'd just read in Dr Orloff's book, now realised there was a much better alternative approach to achieving her goal. Instead of putting herself through the repeated misery of failure, she asked her boyfriend to complete the quest for her. Fifteen minutes later the problem that had made her miserable for weeks was gone and, after returning from the promised pizza, she was happily back playing Runescape.

When I asked Sally what here earliest memory of childhood was, she immediately related in exquisite detail an experience that occurred at nursery when she was just 2 or 3 years old. She told me how one of the carers (she even remembered the young woman's name) had asked a group of children to count a row of colourful cups. When they had finished, they could all have jelly. Sally started to count the cups, but she must have missed the instruction they were to do the counting silently, and she was told off. I didn't dig into the details of what was said to her, or the manner of the admonishment, but I strongly suspect it involved nothing more than a quiet word of caution; the staff at the nursery certainly weren't in the business of manhandling, shouting at, or indeed any form of behaviour that would frighten or humiliate their young charges. Yet whatever was said resulted in uncontrollable tears that lasted long after her uneaten jelly had been cleared from the lunch table. Most of her other early memories have a similar theme—she does something perfectly normal, someone says or does something that upsets her, she burst into tears or reacts in some other way that shows a level of sensitivity well in excess of normal. I know she had many, many happy times at nursery. When I went to pick her up, I often spied on her through a window and watched as she interacted happily with the staff and other toddlers. I find it sad that many of her clearest childhood recollections relate to negative experiences.

It's possible if I'd known back then what I now know about empaths, things would have turned out differently for Sally. But I didn't. How could I? We didn't have the Internet back then, and the condition wasn't described in any parenting manual or advice column I came across. I always thought her over-sensitivity was something she'd grow out of as life toughened her up. As I mentioned earlier, I won't beat myself up over this. However, as I also said, if you recognise this in any of the children you care for, please take it seriously.

8

Travel

I got the travel bug when I hit my mid-teens. I remember back then it was called having 'itchy feet'. The first trip abroad I made on my own was to visit my penfriend in Saarbrucken, Germany. This involved taking a train from Liverpool to London, a bus transfer to Heathrow, check my luggage in, navigate through passport control and then board a flight to Germany. On arrival I would retrieve my luggage before being picked up by my penfriend and her family, the Driers. Although I had travelled abroad on school trips, these had always involved a ferry crossing. I had never been in an airport before. There was no useful guidance I could read up on before leaving, so I only had brief written instruction on how to get from the train station in Euston to the bus that would take me to the airport. The layout of Heathrow terminals was a complete mystery to me, as was how to navigate through the numerous activities I needed to complete before I could board the plane to Saarbrucken. None of this worried me in the slightest. In fact, I was excited by the prospect of doing something grown up all on my own, and I knew I would always be able to find someone who could help me if I had any trouble.

Everything went perfectly. The train arrived on time in Euston. I easily found my transfer bus that delivered me to Heathrow with plenty of time to check my luggage in and then relax in the departure lounge. The only slight hiccup was that all the flights displayed on the overhead boards showed locations such as Aberdeen, Isle of Mann, Guernsey and other locations none of which sounded particularly foreign. But after a quick word with a member of staff who told me I was in the domestic departure lounge, I wandered off to passport control and breezed through the security check. This took me into international departures where the boards reassuringly showed flights to exotic locations, including my flight to Saarbrucken.

As an aside, I have no idea why I had a German penfriend. I had never studied German at school, I spoke not one word of the language, and as far as I remember, I had no desire to learn. I did however have a longing to travel abroad—and to do so on my own. I can only imagine that my penfriend and subsequent trip was organised by my father, who occasionally travelled to the Ford factory at Saar Louis where my penfriend's father worked. Anyway, I don't care too much how or why my trip to stay at the home of hilariously named Herr Drier came about, but it marked the point at which I stepped out of adolescence and, at least temporarily, became an adult. I think I had just turned 16.

This was just one of many trips abroad. When possible, I preferred to travel with friends. A long summer holiday spent bumming around Europe with my university mates, and an unlimited-travel InterRail ticket was definitely a highlight of my wanderlust. When I couldn't persuade friends to travel with me, I would sign up for some madcap holiday, such as a Top Deck tour of Europe on an ancient double-decker bus. A bus that served both as transport and converted to sleeping quarters. Top Deck was an Australian company, and I had the time of my life travelling with twenty or so young people from the southern hemisphere for four glorious, carefree weeks. Although I was a regular traveller in my late teens and early twenties, I never went beyond Western Europe. Eastern Europe was pretty much closed to westerners, and long-haul flights were prohibitively expensive. How things have changed.

As the girls were growing up, we enjoyed a few family holidays abroad, starting with a truly amazing five-day trip to Lapland, where we went in search of Santa and his reindeer on Christmas day. It took a few hours of travelling deep into the snow-covered forest, but with expert guidance from his mischievous elves we eventually discovered Santa's cosy hideaway. Despite having just returned from his around-the-world trip to deliver presents, Santa was extremely hospitable and welcoming—which was a relief, given how excited my girls were to meet him. I was concerned later in the day when I spotted shredded reindeer on the dinner menu. But the staff assured us that Rudolph and his sleigh-pulling companions were completely safe, and enjoying a well-deserved rest in the local forest. They were far too important to find themselves served up on a dinner plate. The following year we spent three weeks over Christmas and New Year in Disneyland Florida, which was the first time any of us had been outside of Europe. This was followed a year later by our only other non-European trip, a holiday in the Dominican Republic. After this three-year blitz, family holidays abroad were suspended as school fees took hold of our finances.

Shortly after Harriet had secured a place at university and started a gap year, she casually announced that she was planning a trip to Africa and Southern Asia with a group of her school friends. They would be away for seven weeks. The list of places they were planning to visit included the dreamy white beaches of Tanzania and the magical island of Zanzibar—the birthplace of my musical hero, Freddie Mercury. Thailand and Egypt were also on the itinerary. Her plans sounded so amazing I struggled to supress my own long-forgotten wanderlust which was threatening to resurface. After a few months intense planning and getting all the requisite jabs, the group of six was nearly ready to go. I had no concerns about travel plans. I knew all her travel companions and their families. I knew they would look out for each other, and if anything bad did happen, everyone would pull together to resolve the problem and get them safely home. The sheer competence of the group was admirably demonstrated a week before they were due to leave when violence broke out in Egypt—their first destination. They hastily abandoned their plans to visit the pyramids and cruise down the Nile, and expertly launched themselves into the job of making alternative arrangements. Using their extensive network of contacts, they secured a ten-day volunteering assignment at Camps International in Kenya, and re-arranged their flights. It seemed as straight forward as if they were just changing the start time and location of a quiz night at a local pub. The entire trip passed by with minimal drama, and it was one relaxed and happy daughter that we picked up from Heathrow at the end of her amazing adventure.

If Harriet's first sortie into the distant southern hemisphere had been gratifyingly stress-free, the same could not be said for Sally's first journey. Shortly after starting life in 6th form, Sally's school began organising a trek to South America, with spaces available for twelve pupils. As fourteen youngsters had applied, the organisers decided that the first two names to be pulled out of a hat would be the unlucky pupils to miss out. None of our family ever wins a raffle when there is a good prize on offer, but of course Sally was one half of those who 'won' the privilege of being told they would not be going. Naturally she was bitterly disappointed, and the fact the draw had been conducted behind closed doors left us wondering whether it had been truly random. But instead of dwelling on how unfair life was, we immediately set to work looking for a better alternative. Within a few days we had found an ideal 2 week conservation programme in Botswana, run by Projects Abroad. In truth, she was much happier with the prospect of spending a fortnight away volunteering with a group of strangers, instead of 18 months of mandatory fund-raising activities, followed by a trip in the company of several people she really didn't like. In the first week after the draw several people who had been selected to go on the school trek dropped out, and Sally was invited to join the group. She was delighted to decline the offer.

The volunteering project she was joining was targeted at 15-18-year-olds. I had assumed there would be a group of young people meeting up at Heathrow, travelling with a Projects Abroad leader to

South Africa and then on to Botswana. This wasn't the case. Instead she was to get on a flight from Heathrow to Johannesburg, retrieve her luggage, navigate her way across a major international airport, check her luggage in once more, before boarding another flight to Polokwane in Botswana. On arrival she would retrieve her luggage and locate the driver who would take her on to the camp site. The prospect of her doing this on her own was nothing short of terrifying for both of us. We had no doubt that arriving alone at a busy airport and having to do a raft of grown up tasks in a specific order would be utterly overwhelming for her.

We were hit by this bombshell just as we were preparing to leave for a fortnight in Turkey, and within a couple of days of returning home from this family holiday she would be off to Botswana. We had to devise a workable plan quickly. In the space of a few short minutes I had come up with five potential options. Plan A; find out if there is anyone else from Projects Abroad going on the same flight. Plan B; find out if anyone else is going on a flight within a few days of Sally's flight and change to that one. Plan C; see what South Africa Airlines could do to help. She was 17 so not a child, but I figured they may be able to offer help for a vulnerable lone traveller. Plan D; book two weeks off work and travel with her. Plan E; cancel the trip—it was too late to rearrange. I had briefly considered a Plan F; let her fend for herself and hope for the best. But this was never a serious option.

So, as David drove us along the motorway to the airport for our flight to the sun, I fired off a few frantic e-mails to investigate plans A, B and C, but I admit to being very concerned. When we arrived at Dalaman airport in Turkey, I was even more concerned when Sally had a panic attack while we were queueing to get through customs. Dalaman is a small airport, and she was travelling with her family. If she couldn't handle this, she had little chance on her own or even with a stranger to escort her. At this point I had a nagging fear that Plan E would be best for everyone, and we should cancel her trip.

A few days after arriving in Turkey I received an email from

Projects Abroad containing excellent news. There was one other young person on the same flight who would be happy to travel with Sally. He had an upmarket London address, and his family name was something you could reasonably expect to find in the European aristocracy listings in publications such as Burke's Peerage. Perfect. Absolutely Fabulously Fabulous. Sally made contact and arranged to meet him at Heathrow. He was slightly younger than her, but he was already well-travelled and had often travelled alone. It was a massive relief, now we could get on and enjoy our holiday in the Turkish sunshine.

The long-awaited day came, and before we left home, we checked and double checked all the important things. Passport. Check. Tickets. Check. Medication. Check. Are you sure? Show me. Check. Then we took her and her boyfriend to Heathrow and checked her bags in with plenty of time to spare. Her travel companion arrived, and honestly the look of utter dejection on the face of Sally's boyfriend was heart wrenching. Her boyfriend at that time was tall and good looking, but along came a much taller, better looking young man who exuded the confidence in keeping with his grand Germanic name. We said our goodbyes before he gallantly whisked Sally off into the depths of Heathrow airport, then onward to Africa for the adventure of a lifetime.

It was a massive relief when she e-mailed me to let me know that her journey had gone well, and she had arrived in Botswana having already met up with other volunteers on the plane from Johannesburg. The only slight problem was her luggage had been delayed and wouldn't be arriving until the following day. It wasn't a big issue and she wasn't the only member of the group affected. Projects Abroad assured them they would be reunited with their luggage the next morning. In the meantime she had a toothbrush and toothpaste in her travel bag as well as enough medication to get her through the night.

My relaxed state didn't last long. The next evening I got an urgent e-mail from her to tell me that although her luggage had turned up, she couldn't find her medication. She was convinced she put it in her bag, but she'd searched through everything and the boxes of tablets weren't there anymore. Please could I call her because she was distressed and had no idea what she should do. I was working away from home when I received the e-mail, 'WHAT THE FUCK, SALLY' I screamed to an empty hotel room. 'HOW COULD YOU FORGET YOUR MEDS???? I asked you if you had them and you told me you did. We checked. We double checked. Then we checked again. HOW COULD YOU POSSIBLY HAVE FORGOTTEN THEM?' I continued, not caring if anyone else in the hotel, or indeed anywhere in the vicinity of Waterloo Station, could hear my desperate rant. A rant that in reality contained far more repetitions and variations of the word 'fuck' than I care to write for fear of causing sensitive readers too much distress. However if you're up for it, and would like to get a real flavour of my actual state of mind at the time, try re-reading the above but add the word 'fucking' nine times, then end with three separate instances of 'fuck', rising in a crescendo, and each punctuated by a short pause.

I said earlier that I'm not capable of anger and I stand by that statement. This explosion of emotion was not born of anger, but of a deep rooted, raw, primal sense of dread. My precious, vulnerable daughter was in a camp site in Botswana, surrounded by strangers, hours away from emergency medical help, and separated from the medication she desperately needed. Not only had I allowed her to go, I had actively encouraged her. What possessed me to believe this could possibly turn out well? I pride myself on being resourceful and being able to resolve problems with the minimum of fuss, but here was a challenge I feared might be beyond me. I was concerned about the consequences if her medication was stopped abruptly. Her psychiatrist had made it abundantly clear that she must not come off it suddenly. 'Shit. What should I do?' I thought. This was an encouraging sign that I had regained my equilibrium. 'Fuck' had been replaced by 'Shit', and I was thinking it not screaming it. Definite progress, and time for action. I called the number Sally had left me. I got through to her without too much delay, and was relieved that she sounded reasonably calm. It turned out she had not forgotten to pack her medication. It had been stolen from her luggage somewhere between checking her bag in at Heathrow and picking it up at Polokwane after it had spent a night 'secured' in an office at the airport. No one else from the group had been targeted. Apparently they had prior experience of travelling to poor countries, and had the foresight to secure their luggage from opportunistic thieves. Sally's backpack was the only item that presented an easy target. I now realised why people go to the trouble of wrapping their luggage in vast quantities of cling film.

A lot of things had been taken, but the thief had showed some compassion by leaving her with one pair of socks, two pairs of knickers, one of her three torches, and two heavy-duty gardening gloves that unfortunately were both left-handed. All her hygiene products were gone, but big items such as her waterproof coat and boots had been spared. She would be able to replace everything she needed through donations from the rest of the group, or by stocking up at the market on their planned visit to the local town a few days later. Everything that is, except her highly valued sense of privacy, which had been painfully and irreparably violated by the thief, and—more importantly—her vital medication.

So Project 'Get Sally's Meds to Botswana' kicked off and, unusually for me, I determinedly took on the role of Project Manager. There were two major issues to resolve. Firstly I needed to source a new supply of tablets as she had none left at home. Secondly I needed to get them to her as quickly as possible. Neither of these was easy. I researched FedEx, Parcelforce Worldwide, DHL, UPS and other international couriers, but no one offered a service that would be delivered before she had left Botswana for her journey home. Getting a new prescription was also a challenge because her psychiatrist was on leave, and the brand she used wasn't available in Africa. But I was a mother on a mission, and nothing was going to get in my way. Within 36 hours, and after countless phone calls, including to the Director of Projects Abroad in Africa, a plan was set into action. It involved her GP faxing a prescription for a suitable alternative brand of meds to a hospital in South Africa. From here they would be picked up by a medic from the Projects Abroad team, who happened to be visiting another young volunteer who was at the hospital having been injured by a machete. The medic planned to take the tablets to Sally, check her over and she would be back on them within 4 days of her last dose. Despite the earlier dire warnings from her psychiatrist, the duration of the gap would not cause her too much of a problem in terms of withdrawal symptoms.

Of all the projects and crazy team-building activities I have been involved with throughout three decades of my career, none has come close to giving me the buzz, the feeling of teamwork, or the sense of achievement that successful completion of Project 'Get Sally's Meds to Botswana' gave me. Projects Abroad, CAMHS Bristol and Sally's GP practice, I salute you. And to the volunteer who was unfortunate enough to be injured by a machete, I sincerely hope you recovered and were able to continue your travels.

9

Employment

Four years after embarking on student life, and armed with my not-exactly-hard-earned Lower Second Class Honours degree in Mechanical Engineering and a now-permanent job at Rolls Royce, my engineering career seemed set fair for a long and fascinating journey towards retirement at the ripe old age of 60. This vision of the future lasted roughly 2 years, when the journey was abruptly diverted after I came across the bright new world of computer programming. The main attraction of this career was it promised good money while satisfying my primitive desire for minimal human contact. Three decades later the world of Information Technology has evolved beyond recognition, but it still proves to have been an excellent career choice.

In addition to providing a solid academic education, university also prepared me to embark on the check-list of activities that were essential components of life as a real grownup. By the time I hit my 30s I was a home-owner, wife and mother. In addition, I was working a 60-hour week and within a whisker of booking myself long term accommodation at Napoleon XIV's funny farm, accompanied by my personal white-coated assistant.

A few years earlier when Harriet was barely out of nappies, I had jumped ship from the Engineering sector that was undergoing an extreme 'belt-tightening' exercise (a euphemism for merciless job cuts). I relaunched my career in Financial Services, which was awash with money, and busy setting the foundations of the innovative assortment of mis-selling scandals that have plagued the industry ever since. *Work hard, play hard, take, take, take* was the undocumented mantra, and companies were slashing tax bills by diverting vast quantities of revenue towards staff training. In the first few years alone I enjoyed a wide range of computing courses and an even wider range of 'soft-skill' training. One such course was a 5-day residential Leadership course. It involved a bunch of strangers driving like maniacs around an otherwise tranquil village near Ross on Wye, with no purpose other than to achieve an arbitrary—and completely unnecessary—goal before anyone else did. Hell that was an intense week.

Other somewhat less extravagant courses focused on team building and self-discovery. One was based on The Seven Habits of Highly Effective People, a book by American guru Steven Covey that taught me many things including, somewhat bizarrely, how to juggle. I'm told the book is still popular today although, as is typical throughout modern life, it is bigger, better and bolder. 7 habits would never be sufficient for a new generation of readers, so a new one was added. Juggling has been replaced by fire-eating. (Note to self: find out what the 8th habit is and check if the statement about fire-eating is true.)

Although this seemed stark raving bonkers at the time, it undoubtedly changed the course of my life away from the nice men in white coats towards becoming a reasonably competent and valued team player, wife, mother and member of the human race. For that I will be eternally grateful.

The main life-enhancing lesson I learned from the personal leadership training was unashamed selfishness. It is doubtful this was the intended outcome of the expensive training funded by my employer, but that's what happened. Suddenly I felt empowered to put my own well-being top of my list of priorities, and to put my family on at least an equal footing as my job. I embraced the emerging trend of 'work-life balance' with all my heart and soul.

The 60 hour weeks stopped. I found countless ways to create sentences that expressed the core sentiment of 'not my problem mate' but in a positive, non-confrontational way. For example, when my manager told me I was needed on site throughout the entire weekend or a vital project milestone would be missed, 'not my problem mate' became 'I'm very sorry, I have other plans this weekend, but I'll be happy to come in for a couple of hours after 5pm on Sunday if that will help.' When my manager demanded for the third time in a week that I spent the night alone in a cold, scary data centre nursing a job through to completion, 'not my problem mate' became 'I'm very sorry, my husband's out tonight so I have to look after my young daughter. But it's OK, because I've written up instructions so someone else on the team can do it.' The formula was simple. Step 1: express regret—'I'm sorry but…' is perfect every time. Step 2: give reason—this can be as inventive as you wish, and any semblance of truth is optional. Step 3: give alternative—a concession or compromise that makes it appear as though you care. There was a downside to this approach. I was documenting my routine tasks to the point that I was making myself less indispensable with every 'I'm sorry but…' Still, it was a price worth paying to get my life back and start enjoying being a mother.

As time went by, there was an increasing drive to outsource IT jobs to India, which brought with it considerable uncertainty and a constant cycle of redundancies. Initially this was unsettling because I hated the idea of losing my cushy job. But my concern passed as soon as I realised I had the uncanny ability to make myself temporarily indispensable whenever it suited me.

The dawn of outsourcing coincided with an epidemic of short-term thinking led by management consultants. They knew their tenure was short, and would be long gone before shareholders realised they'd spent millions of pounds on projects that hadn't delivered the promised benefits. Working with management consultants was immensely enjoyable, in particular the regular opportunities it provided to indulge in a round of Bullshit Bingo. Just in case you've not heard of the game, Bullshit Bingo resembles regular bingo in that everyone gets a personalised card, but numbers are replaced by a random selection of the latest Management Consultant Speak. Tried, trusted but meaningless phrases such as 'push the envelope', 'sweat the assets', 'helicopter view', 'kick the tyres on the cadillac' and many, many more. Whenever a consultant uttered one of the phrases on your card, you marked it off and—just like regular bingo—the winner was the person who was first to cross off a complete line.

Always keen to learn new skills, I taught myself enough management bullshit to create a special set of 'not my problem mate' responses, including such gems as 'I'm sorry but that's a real paradigm shift and I don't have the bandwidth to drill down and elucidate the granular insight required. I suggest you touch base with the product evangelist who's been involved cradle-to-grave.' Pure quality.

Looking back over my career, there have been few stand-out achievements. Certainly nothing where I can say—hand on heart—I had a positive impact on the life of another. Maybe if you have ever switched your ISA provider to get a better savings rate, I can justifiably claim a smidgen of the credit. But that's as good as it gets. I have always been a small cog in an extremely large machine. I don't mean this negatively as it has generally suited me perfectly. Once I'd escaped from the 60-hour weeks, I encountered very little stress in my working life, which was surprising because throughout the nineties and well into the naughties the 'blame culture' was rife. Although I had an important role in whatever small team I was working in, I always managed to avoid finding myself in the direct firing line. I can't be sure if this was because I'd developed a totally unfounded—but useful—reputation as 'a crazy scouse git you don't want to piss off'. Alternatively it may simply have been that other teams could always be counted on to screw up earlier and more visibly than my own team.

So after a difficult period during my late twenties and early thirties, I achieved the Gen X dream of work-life balance. Presumably as a consequence of being happy with my well-balanced life and work, I was able to avoid quitting my job, packing my bags and buggering off to the Franklin River in Tasmania to indulge myself in a well-deserved mid-life crisis scuba diving in search of duck-billed platypus. The same is true of David, my husband. The first 20 years of his working life weren't exactly bliss. But since returning to work after a decade-long stint as a house husband, David now has an enjoyable and stress-free job, and is looking forward to continuing in the same line of work until he retires at a time of his choosing.

Harriet wants to take a different approach to her journey through employment. Like many of her Millennial peers, she is in search of *work-life harmony*, and it's a search which starts early. In fact the search for work-life harmony appears to be the Millennial's approach to avoiding a mid-life crisis by bringing it forward 20 years or so and calling it a quarter-life crisis. The underlying philosophy is that by understanding and exploring what you want from your working life early on, you avoid the mistakes made by previous generations that led to vast numbers of us oldies enduring long periods of work-induced misery. Until recently, a large part of Harriet's efforts in life—education, sport and career progression—have been focused on what was expected of her. Expectations crafted by her parents, her school and society in general. Expectations that made her miserable.

Now, she is taking the time out to explore her creative side, before getting too entrenched in her working life. She wants to be her own boss, and is attempting to develop a profitable business doing something she loves. However, she is pragmatic and knows there will come a point in the next few years where earning a respectable and reliable income will take on a higher priority than enjoying her work. If her nascent business fails to provide the level of income she wants, she accepts she will need to support herself with a 'proper job' while continuing her business in parallel. Part of her time now is focused on identifying the perfect 'proper job'. One that uses the skills and qualifications gained from her first 25 years of life, along with the skills she is developing now and—most importantly—her growing self-awareness of what makes her truly happy. That's what work-life harmony is all about.

Harriet seems to be following a path that was predicted a decade ago when she was 16. Not the path her parents or school or society in general expected from her, but one that was suggested by a questionnaire she completed as part of her school's careers guidance. It appears we may have been unfairly critical of the questionnaire, which came to the utterly ridiculous conclusion that Harriet—along with many of her equally high-achieving friends—was well suited to being a florist. A FLORIST!!! Seriously, all the expensive education and endless misery-inducing revision just to prepare her for a career as a florist. Get real. Sorry florists out there, but does it even count as a career? Well, what's Harriet now choosing to do in the early stages of her quarter-life crisis? Not quite a florist, but she is painting flowers on her self-crafted wooden bread boards.

Careers advice at school seemed a hit and miss affair. The same questionnaire that surprisingly may have proved spot on for Harriet, was definitely well off the mark for Sally. High on its list of recommendations for her was a Police Officer—one of the worst jobs for someone with social anxiety. Either Sally was untruthful in her answers, or the questionnaire failed to take into account her mental health. I'll go with the latter.

When Sally became ill, I wasn't prepared for how abruptly and forcefully she was pushed off her designated trail, falling face-first into a deep ditch overgrown with thick, thorny brambles that engulfed her fragile body. My natural reaction was to frantically pull her back up and, regardless of her protestations of exhaustion and searing pain, get her back on the path. Time was of the essence. She mustn't miss out. Education. Education. Education. That's the mantra from the Government, the education system, employers and society in general. Throughout my entire life I had been brainwashed into believing that qualifications and tertiary education are the ONLY way to make it in life. There is no other option. Everything else is failure.

Once I'd accepted that Sally wasn't going off to university to follow on her pre-ordained path of a degree, followed by a well-paid career, I started to investigate the alternatives open to a previously bright young adult, whose brain had been dulled by the effects of medication, and who genuinely could not function much before 10am. On many days she was incapable of functioning at all. Even on the days which started full of energy, there was no guarantee an unexpected loud bang or unwelcome encounter with an old acquaintance, wouldn't turn the rest of her day very bad indeed. Again I turned to Google for answers. 'What are good careers for people with anxiety and depression?' I asked hopefully. A list was returned. 'No Google, I asked for *careers* not *jobs.* Please try again.' Same result. Clearly Google doesn't recognise the difference between a long term fulfilling career and a repetitive, albeit blissfully stress-free, job. After investigating the first few links I began to fear that Sally was destined for a life stacking supermarket shelves in the dead of night. I must admit this was a heart-breaking scenario and not what I had hoped for. As usual, my pessimism was only temporary, and as I dug deeper into the more interesting links, I realised there are plenty of fulfilling careers open to her without a full set of A-levels or a university degree. Some—such as accountant, computer programmer, lab technician or professional dog behaviourist—required training and the ability to interact with others; while talent and the energy for self-promotion are the foundations for success in other more solitary options, such as writer, photographer or artist. In the early days of her illness we decided to give writing and photography a try. We invested in a good camera, a new laptop and online training courses she could dip in and out of whenever she felt up to it. Sadly she never felt up to it, and apart from taking hundreds of photos of Rupert, her new dog, she got little use out of any of the purchases. It now turns out we may have been on the right track, it was just too much, too soon.

Of course what Sally needed was to be helped—with patience and great care—out of her brambled-infested ditch, but not back onto the old path from which she had fallen. Instead she needed a quiet, stress-free place where she could rest and focus what little energy she had on her recovery.

There's no annex to the rule-book of parenthood that explains how to reconcile your child's mental illness with their need—whether real or perceived—for qualifications. If such a tome exists, I've never found it. Neither have I come across career guidance for young people with mental illness. No specialist careers officer. No questionnaires. Nothing. You have to write your own. With the benefit of hindsight, I'd encourage the very first sentence of the very first page to shout out 'FORGET ABOUT EDUCATION. FORGET ABOUT CAREERS. They can wait. FOCUS ON GETTING BETTER!!!!!'

It took a long time for that particular truth to sink in. When it did, it was liberating. I stopped looking at Sally's time away from education as lost, or wasted, or other such negative term. Instead, I took on board the immortal words of Ralph Waldo Emerson—'*life is a journey, not a destination*'. Sally is on a different journey to the one we'd planned, one that is undoubtedly a far greater challenge, as it has meant navigating difficult and entirely unfamiliar landscapes. Less a journey, more an exploration through hostile territories. Another long-held truth I clung to was '*that which does not kill us, makes us stronger*', from the German Philosopher, Friedrich Nietzsche. Once I'd started thinking in these terms, positives came scurrying out from the undergrowth. Positives such as she was developing a real understanding of herself; what 'makes her tick'; what is important to her; her strengths and weaknesses. I was well into my 30s before I gave any serious consideration to these essential foundations of a happy and successful life. Positives such as learning from an early age an array of essential tools for dealing with (or indeed avoiding) extreme stress and anxiety—skills that will be invaluable on her journey through life, particularly should she ever choose to resume formal education and enter a traditional career.

I'll freely admit that having 2 minimally employed daughters both in their 20s was never part of my life plan, but for now I'm happy to put them to work getting this book ready for publication.

Sally is artistic director responsible for the book cover while Harriet is using her social media expertise to develop a marketing plan. It's fun having them around working together on our family project. Maybe one day they'll settle on a career and get a 'proper' job which makes them happy. But even if they decide that's not right for them, I'm confident they'll both emerge from their individual challenges with a rounded set of skills and experience they can use to earn a living. Ideally before the Bank of Mum and Dad files for bankruptcy!

10

Dogs and Other Animals

There was a big empty, dog-shaped hole in my young life. I dreamt of sun-filled days strolling through the park with my faithful companion trotting happily by my side, distracted only by the constant attention from an army of adoring followers (the dog's, not mine). Unfortunately, my parents had a long—and in their view compelling—laundry list of reasons why I couldn't fulfil this fantasy. In summary, they considered dogs to be expensive, time-consuming, messy poop machines that pee on the furniture and dig up the plants. They dismissed as irrelevant the positives such as the love and happiness they bring. I reluctantly accepted their decision with all the grace I could muster, and implemented Plan B instead. If I couldn't have my own, I could at least get a regular fix of canine contact through early morning trips to the local newsagent. Here I could engage in doggie conversations with local Old English Sheep Dogs, Saint Bernards, Chow Chows and a whole assortment of indistinguishable mutts. Sometimes these conversations would even involve the dog's owner.

The subject of getting a dog resurfaced on occasions. It was usually accompanied by increasingly desperate threats to leave home if my parents didn't take my brother to the RSPCA rescue centre and trade him in for a dog. Any dog, I really didn't care. I was certain it was a win-win solution. The world would be a much safer place if the pure evil son they had spawned was secured in a cage and fed through the bars with little risk to human life. In exchange we would take on their most difficult stray, which would surely be easier to live with. In truth, I believe the real reason they didn't want a dog was they secretly feared that my brother would treat any pet with the same anatomical curiosity with which he treated my favourite teddy bear. Although Mum's ability with a needle and thread was good enough to return a stuffed toy to perfect health after a botched tonsillectomy, the challenge of repairing the damage caused by a similar procedure on a living creature would surely prove too great.

As life trundled on, my need for a dog diminished. By the time I entered Motherhood I had adopted a similar, although less extreme, mantra to my parents when the inevitable pleas for canine companionship started. I have no doubt 'Mama' was the first recognisable word uttered by both daughters, but the next? I couldn't be sure if it was 'Papa' or 'Puppy'.

I still loved dogs, but with both myself and my husband in full time work, and with no local support network of family or friends, a resident dog was simply not a viable option. Instead, our first efforts to accommodate pets in the family were focused on a tank of stick insects and a Tamagotchi, the small alien species that deposited an egg on Earth to see what life was like, and were being sneaked into primary school classrooms in all corners of the modern world.

Our first real pet was an eye-wateringly expensive 3-year-old migrant from Slovenia, a tortoise we named Heather. She was an excellent fit to our primary requirement for low maintenance—in particular during her annual hibernation when we put her in a box and ignored her for 4 months. Other than nearly drowning when emerging from her first hibernation (in later years the box was placed in a cupboard instead of a shelf directly above the toilet), she caused minimal drama and a whole heap of entertainment. She loved to explore the ballrooms and paddocks of Princess Barbie Castle, but nothing got her as excited as when the electric lawnmower came out. No sooner had we switched it on for the first cut of spring, than she would start a determined sprint across the garden towards it (and yes tortoises can get up speed), before directing her pent-up sexual frustration at the object of her desire.

The only sticky moment came when we discovered a dark discolouration in her mouth that persisted over several days. Doctor Google advised it could be mouth rot, a potentially fatal disease if left untreated. Somewhere in the process of booking an appointment the word 'tortoise' morphed into 'tortoiseshell cat', and she was ushered into the examination room by a confused young vet who admitted to having no real experience of 'exotics'. We eventually managed to persuade Heather to open her mouth, and after a quick sniff, the vet announced there was no telltale smell that would normally accompany mouth rot. She then questioned me on what I fed her. 'Well just normal tortoise food…lettuce, chopped apples, tomatoes, and her favourites…Oh…Shit…You don't think it could be stains from the bucket loads of deep red and purple petunias she steals from the flower bed do you?' And so it turned out. Heather was given a clean bill of health, and as I placed her in her travel box for the journey home, I'll swear I saw her flash me a mischievous wink and utter a single word. 'Sucker'. But more of my hallucinations later.

Some years later we ventured into the world of small furry animals with the purchase of gerbils. Fizz, Smudge and Lily were 3 sisters who we were assured could be housed in a single cage. Life away from the trained pet shop staff didn't start too well for Fizz who was accidentally flung across her new home after clamping her tiny-but razor-sharp-teeth to Sally's finger. We then spent the entire evening trying to encourage a traumatised Fizz out from under Sally's bed, before finally capturing her and returning her to her anxious sisters. After this excitement, gerbil life calmed down for a long time until the day that sister turned on sister. At 6am one morning while working away from home, I was awakened by a phone call from Sally, who sounded distraught. In between sobs, she explained how Smudge had gouged out one of Lily's eyes, and Lily was now lying in a pool of her own blood while her sisters performed satanic rituals and feasted on her brains. OK, maybe the last part resulted from a combination of my over-active imagination and the fact it was 6 o'clock in the morning, but it certainly sounded as though disturbing events had occurred over night. I was never sure why Sally phoned me that morning, rather than summoning her father who was in bed about 3 meters away from where the carnage was unfolding. I guess sometimes only mothers are good enough. Happily the reality of the sibling dispute was not as dramatic as I had imagined, and all 3 sisters survived the incident with only minor damage. Nevertheless it was clear that they could no longer live together, so we purchased a new cage, exiled Lily for her own protection, and life continued without further drama.

Shortly after Sally started treatment for her mental health problems, subliminal forces set to work breaking down my reluctance to enter the world of dog ownership. There was no obvious trigger, just a gradual acceptance that it was now not only practical but also the right thing to do. I explored the enormous body of literature that extols the benefits, both mental and physical, of regular contact with dogs. From full-blown scientific studies that prove levels of serotonin—the brain's happy chemical—increase during petting sessions, to heart-warming stories taken from real-life. Stories such as the bond between young Owen Hoskins and Haatchi, a 3-legged Anatolian Shepherd. If you don't know this story, do yourself a favour and check it out.

By the time Sally officially dropped out of school, all my reluctance had evaporated and I felt ready to take the plunge. We agreed that we would get a dog from a rescue centre, then we drew up a checklist of essential and preferred characteristics. We wanted a house-trained, medium-sized dog that didn't leave long hairs all over the furniture. One that didn't bark excessively, was sociable with people and other dogs, could be left alone for a few hours and ideally was lazy. Not too much to ask. With Harriet working in the fund raising department at the Bristol Cats & Dogs Home, this was the obvious place to start our search. Their website was full of profiles of gorgeous Huskies (an unfortunate by-product of the popularity of Game of Thrones). There was also an army of not so gorgeous (but still lovable) cross breeds of unknown parentage, but invariably described as Staffy-X. Of the available dogs, only 2 met our strict selection criteria, both from the Staffy-X stable, and both 'longing to meet their forever families'. Luckily both dogs needed to go to separate homes, so there was never any chance we might 'accidentally' sign up to take them both home with us.

Our first choice was Rupert, a 10-month-old Staffador (Staffy/Labrador cross). Within seconds of meeting 2 became 1 as Rupert and Sally effortlessly mind-melded and merged their DNA. For my part, I have to admit to being a little disappointed by his colouring and muscular stature. My first impression—and it is difficult to admit this even now—was that he looked like an enormous turd. OK, I've said it and I've been forgiven by the people who matter most. Move on. Appearance aside, my only real concern was that he suffered from dysplasia of the hips, which was likely to be life limiting and, as an existing condition, uninsurable. However, we agreed that we would give him an amazing quality of life while he was still fit and healthy, and deal with problems if they arise.

Rupert settled comfortably into family life and developed a good, if somewhat mischievous, relationship with Heather the tortoise. They could often be seen sitting together on the patio, looking for all the world as if they were in deep and meaningful conversation. Rupert liked to tease Heather by gently picking up her lettuce, walking thirty metres across the garden before dropping it and returning to her side. The whole process took Rupert no more than a few seconds, but for a short-legged tortoise retrieving lunch was a marathon journey she never bothered to complete. She got her own back on at least one occasion when she was seen skulking suspiciously towards Rupert's rear end. Then, while he dozed, she nipped the tip of his tail before retreating to the safety of her cage. There's definitely something about that animal I haven't figured out.

Introducing Rupert into our lives helped me re-discovered what I instinctively knew as a child; that dogs can act as a proxy for conversation with absolutely anyone. On one occasion while standing with Sally in a queue in Pets at Home, I noticed that the face of the man in front of us was covered with tattoos of scorpions. I am ashamed to admit that under normal circumstances, I would make a snap judgment that this was not a person I wished to acknowledge. Then, regardless of how inconvenient or impolite, I would take whatever action was necessary to avoid eye contact. But to my amazement, I watched as Sally expertly engaged in conversation with the Man with the Scorpion Face through the adorable and well-behaved puppy that accompanied him. With complete disregard for her usual shyness, she initiated the 2-step protocol I had used so effectively myself all those years ago at my local newsagents. Step 1: use any acceptable means of getting the dog's attention. Step 2: engage the dog in conversation. Something along lines of 'Oooh, you're such a sweetie[8]. Yes you are. What's your name?' is a reliable opener. These 2 simple steps invariably lead to immediate removal of conversational barriers between protocol initiator (shy person) and protocol target (dog owner), leading to meaningful and natural conversation. Sometimes even with full-on eye contact between the two participants. Bravo Sally!

As time passed, Sally's mental health showed no signs of sustained improvement, and she spent much of her time curled up on the sofa with Rupert, watching Super Vet, playing mindless computer games or expanding Rupert's repertoire of tricks. As well as using the computer for games, she was also working her way through countless YouTube videos from the Cesar Millan Dog Whisperer series. Millan is a Mexican-born resident of the United States who has achieved great celebrity in the field of dog behaviour. Several years after entering the US as a 21-year-old illegal immigrant who spoke no English, Millan created the Dog Psychology Centre which specialized in rehabilitating aggressive dogs. Through her endless hours of 'research' Sally learnt many tips and techniques that

8 If the dog's sex is obvious, you can get extra kudos by swapping 'sweetie' for 'good boy/girl' as appropriate. But if you're not sure, etiquette suggests it's best to avoid taking a chance.

helped integrate Rupert into our daily lives.

Sally's growing interest in the subject of dog behaviour—and her obvious affinity with members of the canine world—led us to consider the possibility of a dog-related career. Previously she had spent time helping out at the canine hydrotherapy centre where Rupert went for his fortnightly swim. Unfortunately her involvement didn't last long. The routine of getting up at the crack of dawn and dragging herself to the bus stop, before spending an exhausting day on her feet, proved too much for her. Options were limited owing to the joint constraints that she was unable to get up in the mornings, unable to drive, constantly exhausted and frequently in the grip of debilitating anxiety. But none of these obstacles ruled out doggie day care. What if we could find clients who would drop their pooches off with us on their way to work and then pick them up again on their way home? All Sally would have to do would be get out of bed, safely negotiate her sleepy body down stairs before the first visitor arrived, then spend the day looking after a few carefully selected, adorable dogs. And so Love My Dog At Home came into existence. Armed with the necessary council approval, pet insurance, first aid and health & safety certificates, a newly laid wooden floor and all manner of other essentials, we opened our home to an assortment of dogs who came either for day care or for extended holidays. Our secure, reasonably sized garden became a doggie play (and poop) ground. Our large log cabin was renamed 'dog cabin' and re-purposed from its previous role as my office into luxury accommodation for our canine guests.

In August 2016 we welcomed Gretel—a graceful and agile refugee from Romania—as our first paying guest. Earlier I described our garden as secure, and it was certainly secure in that the plodding, muscular form of Rupert stood no chance of escape. Gretel was nothing like Rupert, but had many characteristics of the urban foxes who effortlessly find their way into and out of our 'secure' garden. So we had to make a few rapid modifications to ensure her first day with us wasn't her last.

Gretel became a regular, and established herself as a strict but caring maternal figure who kept the more energetic, young dogs in check. Over the course of ten months we looked after twenty or so different dogs of varying shapes, sizes and temperaments. Rupert got on reasonably well with most of them, in particular those who were willing to spend countless hours playing tug with him. But there were also a few who made him fearful. One source of extreme anxiety came in the form of Bear, an adorable, enormous, 6-month-old ball of energy. Bear's owners had thought they were getting a husky. They'd done plenty of research, visited the breeders and seen both the husky parents before taking young Bear home with them. No one knows if it was the Bristol air, or a rogue gene bestowed on his blood line many generations earlier by a malamute ancestor, but Bear grew and grew until he reached the size of a Shetland pony. He was my idea of a perfect dog. Rupert didn't share my enthusiasm and made his feelings clear by cowering in the corner of the room, while Bear spread his enormous, pure white body across Rupert's bed. For the sake of Rupert's mental health, sadly Bear had to go.

My work schedule meant I was often around to help Sally out, and we shared many happy hours together walking and playing with the dogs. We also spent weekends away, learning about the causes of dog aggression and how to deal with it. But despite the great array of positives, there was no getting away from the fact that Sally often found looking after dogs could be extremely hard work. They wanted to play, go out for walks and all the other normal things that dogs want to do, but often all Sally wanted to do was sleep. The reality was there were many times when she had no choice, and falling into a deep, medication-induced sleep was all she was capable of. It was also very, very stressful. Dogs don't always get on—either with each other or with humans. They don't always come back when called—preferring instead to wriggle under barriers into spaces that are not accessible to their larger, less agile human carers. They seem to think this is hilarious. Sally didn't. Without question, she loved all the dogs she cared for, but this regular inconsiderate behaviour would make her anxious and tearful. Eventually, for the sake of Sally's mental health, Love My Dog At Home closed its doors and our doggie adventure ended. For a while Rupert missed his assortment of canine companions, but he gradually settled back into his earlier persona as a loveable, but somewhat grumpy, loner.

11

Mysteries of the Brain

I mentioned earlier that Mum has been harbouring a dark, uncomfortable secret. A secret that, but for a chance conversation, she may have taken with her to the grave. Well, it transpires that for several years she has heard voices and music she is certain aren't real. One morning while lying awake in bed planning the day ahead, she was surprised to hear the rich voice of a baritone singing Italian opera accompanied by a full orchestra. She was even more surprised when she confirmed that her radio was switched off, and there was no obvious external source. The music stayed with her for about 5 minutes as she walked around the house, trying to locate the massed ranks of talented musicians. She looked out the window, but no sign of the baritone or orchestra in her garden or anywhere else on her quiet suburban road. Convinced that the music was not real, she jumped full-on into Ockham's Razor principle, which postulates that if all other things are equal, simpler explanations are generally better than more complex ones. In accordance with this tried and tested medieval philosophy, she concluded she must be going bonkers.

This, along with numerous similar experiences, only came to light after I had made one of my infrequent trips to Liverpool, and spent the night in my childhood bedroom. The next morning I mentioned to Mum that at about 2am and again at 4am (more about my insomnia later) I'd heard people chatting in one of the local gardens. It wasn't loud or annoying; I was just surprised given it was a cold, wet and thoroughly miserable December night. Not for one moment did I doubt the voices were real. As a long-term resident of an area with a high density of students and young people, I am well used to parties that go on into the early hours of the morning. My observation triggered Mum into pushing open the door marked 'Private' and revealing the presence of the musicians who had taken up residence within the confines of her head. She had no idea these upmarket cranial squatters existed until they rewarded her unknowing hospitality with glorious performances of excerpts from Puccini's Tosca.

Rather than accepting Mum's self-diagnosis of borderline insanity, her story reminded me of several long-forgotten case studies I had read in a book called *The Man Who Mistook His Wife for a Hat*, written by Dr Oliver Sacks, a world-renowned neurologist. To be honest, with such an intriguing title, I suspect I would have read the book even if it had been written by Enid Blyton. His thoroughly enjoyable accounts of patients lost in bizarre neurological disorders provide a fascinating insight into the mysteries of human consciousness. In one chapter—*Reminiscence*—he recounted the touching stories of two ladies, both in their eighties, whose experiences were strikingly similar to what Mum had encountered. During the course of their auditory hallucinations, the patients were plugged into electroencephalograms to record their brain activity. Both ladies showed heightened activity in their temporal lobes—regions associated with the representation of sounds and music. Subsequent brain scans showed they had suffered minor strokes in the area, confirming that their hallucinations did indeed have a physical cause. Mum is now reassured that although there are unusual shenanigans going on in her head, she is not possessed by a high-quality orchestra, and neither is she going bonkers.

Back to the voices which triggered Mum's revelation—the ones I experienced during my stay in Liverpool. At the time I assumed the voices were real and belonged to a group of Liverpudlians who had good reason to spend the night outside in the cold. Perhaps they were chain smokers who were banned from lighting-up indoors. Yes, that's probably it—a simple explanation, and a good fit with the philosophy of William, the monk from Occam. But what if the voices I heard were not real, but instead emanated from the expanding voids within my head where my short-term memory used to reside? It got me thinking of three separate occasions in the past when I clearly recall experiencing a few bars of enchanting, melodic—but completely inexplicable—music. There were no other anomalies or symptoms accompanying the episodes which lasted just a few seconds, and many years separated each one. These aren't my only experiences of what I'll call *wakeful weirdness*, neither are they the most interesting. At various point throughout my life I have experienced events which—by most measures—would be considered strange. Events that have been a source of intrigue rather than a cause for concern. Now—at the risk of initiating a chain of events that starts with a government psychologist concluding I am a danger to myself and the world in general, and ends with me being locked up in a secure unit for the insane—I will relate three of the most noteworthy of these experiences.

Firstly, when I was on a school trip to York Minster, I had just had my photograph taken when I felt a strong jolt on my shoulder, which resulted in me falling down several stone steps. I was certain there was no one close enough to have been responsible for the push, and the friend who had taken the photo confirmed this. The event occurred around the peak of my anti-religion rebellion, and it crossed my mind that maybe it was a sign from 'on high', symbolising my fall from grace. But as soon as the thought had completed its short and rapid journey, the logical part of my brain stepped in with the more sensible suggestion that I had suffered a muscle spasm in my shoulder, which had fooled my entire central nervous system into believing I had been pushed.

The second incident occurred when Harriet was a toddler. I was playing with one of her musical books that matched pictures of farmyard animals to the sounds they make. You know the type—press the picture of a cow, and the book rewards you with a realist 'moo'. (The reason I was playing with Harriet's book has been lost in the mists of time. I don't know where she was right then, but I'm certain she wasn't with me.) Anyway, on this otherwise normal evening, when I pressed one of the buttons—for the sake of argument let's go with the pig—instead of returning a realistic 'oink' the book launched into 'Old Macdonald had a farm, E-I-E-I-O.' Frustratingly it didn't continue by informing me what was on his farm, it just returned to the beginning of the line, stuck in an infuriating loop. The words were sung in an American accent while a fiddler played at break-neck speed in the background. Very Country and Western. This continued for a good few minutes. I tried pushing every conceivable combination of buttons, shaking the damn thing, and even manically screaming at it to shut up. The book eventually fell silent after I successfully suffocated it—along with its resident demonic version of John Denver—under a thick, comforting, feather-down pillow. The next time I summoned up the courage to press the pig button it obliged—rather apologetically—with an 'oink'. As before, my immediate suspicion that the universe was misbehaving was soon replaced by the more logical explanation that there was a temporary blip in the book's electronic circuits, which had triggered playback of one of its multitude of hidden recordings.

Finally, and the most intriguing of all, the strange case of the phantom traffic lights...This story relates to a tricky local road junction I often have to find my way across. What makes this intersection challenging is poor visibility of on-coming traffic as it emerges from behind a row of houses. If everyone kept even marginally below twice the speed limit, there would plenty of time to make it safely to the other side without drama. But for whatever reason, occasionally a motorist feels the need for speed, and comes tearing into view at an inopportune moment. Personally, I have never suffered a collision, or even a close-call, but I have witnessed a few unpleasant accidents there. So I was delighted when I found out that a set of traffic lights had been installed to make the junction safe. While travelling home later that evening I was excited to experience the new crossing in action, and finally be able to enjoy a stress-free crossing. But when I reached the location, I was shocked to find it looked exactly the same as it had for the preceding decade—there was no sign of the new set of traffic lights or changes to the road layout. The reason I consider this to be the most intriguing of my wakeful weirdness experiences is it is the only one I have been unable to find a rational explanation for. Nothing makes sense. I am certain I didn't 'see' the traffic lights in a dream. I am equally certain that Bristol City Council didn't erect a set of lights, make complex changes to the intersection—including re-painting the markings on a busy main road—then tear the whole lot down and return everything to its original state. All within a 24-hour period. Why would they? A prank? Unlikely. Even the most competent and well- funded council, or the most motivated team from DIY SOS would surely have failed to complete a complex set of tasks in such a short period of time, even if they had worked flat out through the night. Somehow a downright fraudulent event wormed its way into my head and masqueraded as real. If it hadn't been so blatantly fake, it may have remained as a false memory for the rest of my life. In all probability many less extravagant imposters were more successful at sneaking under my sense-check radar, and are now so well integrated into my memory bank it is unlikely they will ever be exposed as interlopers.

I accepted long ago that my brain is easily fooled and not the best interpreter of reality. The televised antics of Derren Brown along with a close-up, table-side performance from another rather amazing magician whose name evades me, have offered regular reinforcement of my brain's shortcomings. Events such as these are comforting as they provide ample evidence I am far from alone in having a brain that struggles with reality. On the contrary. It appears that the tendency to malfunction from time to time is a normal feature in the control centre of standard humans. I'm OK with my brain exactly as it is. I'm truly grateful for its existence and for the amazing things it does for me every second of the day. Maybe it makes a few mistakes and I see and hear things that aren't real—so what? I can live with that. Mum is happy when her orchestra performs an impromptu private concert for her, although she is less thrilled when it is her other occasional visitor, '*the man with a loud voice who sings annoying modern songs*'. Similarly, for many of Dr Sacks' patients who experience auditory hallucinations, the symptoms become an enjoyable and comforting part of their lives. If I ever succumb to the condition, I hope it is music from Queen's A Night at the Opera that plays out in my head, rather than an excerpt from Dad's early years of tuneless violin torture.

When I returned from work one evening, Sally excitedly announced she had discovered why she was easily distracted from non-critical tasks. Tasks such as tidying her bedroom, which had taken on the appearance of a municipal rubbish tip that had been subjected to an extended bombing campaign, before the waste of an entire nation had been distributed haphazardly across the resulting rubble. More evidence daughter number 2 is my clone.

Sorry I digress. Let's get back to Sally's light bulb moment. Firing up YouTube, she clicked on a video entitled *Tim Urban: Inside the mind of a master procrastinator* from TED Talks, an amazing series of educational presentations. Forty hilarious and enlightening minutes later, I had a much better awareness of the internal workings of the human brain, and I now understood the root of her problem. If you want the full details of Mr Urban's work I suggest you head straight to YouTube, but here's a summary. Sally has an Instant Gratification Monkey living in her brain that is much more devious and cunning than most, and adept at outsmarting her Rational Thinker. Another occupier of her brain—and the only resident with the power to exert any control over the Instant Gratification Monkey—the Panic Monster, appears to have gone AWOL a long time ago. All very obvious really. And to think I had once assumed her problem was a direct result of pure idleness.

Want to find out how the brains of procrastinators work?
Watch Tim Urban here.

I myself am not a procrastinator, but a dedicated follower of my own slightly tailored version of the 80:20 rule. Once I've decided to do something, I get on and do it until I have completed about eighty percent of the job when I have a tendency to lose interest, stop and move on to something else. I've found from experience that eighty percent is often enough—as long as I make sure the most important stuff gets done first. As it happens, I'm anticipating using my 80:20 approach for this book. So don't be too surprised if the later chapters are presented in the form of bullet points, littered with grammatical errors, spelling mistakes and statements I haven't bothered to verify. But that's OK. Good enough is good enough. Perfectionists may want to put this book down now and return it for a refund of the missing twenty percent.

But again I digress. While reflecting on Mr Urban's detailed thesis on the workings of the human brain, I couldn't help wondering whether the Instant Gratification Monkey's influence extended beyond procrastination, and into the realm of unhealthy excesses. For example, like most people I am fully aware that if I drink too much, I will wake up with a hangover. It's simple cause and effect, a concept understood since the dawn of modern humans. I also know with certainty that I really, really don't like waking up with a hangover. It sucks. Without doubt, my rational brain is conscious of these facts, and always does its level best to prevent me from drinking too much. Yet, until it eventually grew a pair of balls and asserted its authority, my rational brain was far too weak to resist the pressure from whatever was telling me not to worry, another drink won't hurt you. I now wonder if that was the work of the Instant Gratification Monkey, or even his malevolent twin. The good news is that my rational brain eventually succeeded in capturing the offending primate, placing it in shackles and banishing it to a secure dark dungeon where it has remained for many years with no chance of parole.

Back in Chapter 7 I covered the role mirror neurons may have played in Sally's mental illness. Now, refreshed and rested, I'm ready to embark on a leisurely stroll through another rapidly advancing area of research into anxiety and depression. It's a journey which provides a fascinating glimpse into the world of *trans-poo-sion*. You should know me well enough by now to realise that I couldn't possibly come across a word such as this on the BBC website and let it pass by without further investigation—particularly when the article relates to mental health. Trans-poo-sion is just another word for *faecal transplant*. The word is often written without the hyphens, which I feel doesn't have quite the same initial impact, but is fine for subsequent use. Whichever version you prefer, I'm sure you'll agree they're both much more engaging than good old *faecal transplant*. Transpoosion has been around for quite some time as a treatment (and sometimes even a cure) for illnesses such as Irritable Bowel Syndrome (IBS). It works on the premise that many sufferers of illnesses related to the large intestine have a limited range of bacteria living in their gut. This is a bad thing. It's like living in a society of benign pacifists; at first glance it might appear to be Utopia, but just wait until the gang of out-of-town miscreants comes along to stir things up, and you've got no one with the balls to stand up and fight them off. Like society in general, the strength of your large intestine comes from the diversity of its inhabitants. An increasingly promising treatment for IBS is to introduce an army of bacterial buddies from the poop of a healthy individual, into the digestive system of a sufferer. There are several ways of achieving this, most of which are nowhere near as gross as you are no doubt imagining.

'BUT WHAT'S ANY OF THIS GOT TO DO WITH MENTAL HEALTH?' I hear you screaming. Well, here's what. In a paper[9] published in March 2017 in *Science Translational Medicine*, researchers from McMaster University in Ontario, Canada, harvested stool samples from a healthy group of individuals and two groups of long-term IBS sufferers. Members of one IBS group also suffered anxiety-related disorders common with the disease, while the other group was anxiety-free. Samples were transplanted into happy, germ-free mice and the researchers observed their behaviour. The purpose of the test was two-fold: to confirm that mice with stool samples from both groups of IBS sufferers would themselves develop symptoms of the disease, while those from the healthy group would not; and to determine whether the mice with the samples from the anxious group of IBS sufferers would also go on to develop symptoms of anxiety. Long and short of it is that the tests succeeded on both fronts, as perfectly summarised in the graphic below.

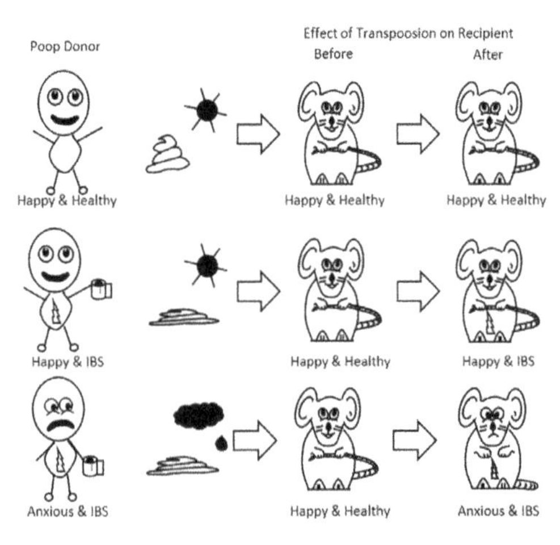

Figure 1 – Effect of Transpoosion on Healthy Mice

9 https://www.the-scientist.com/?articles.view/articleNo/48678/title/Human-Gut-Microbe-Transplant-Alters-Mouse-Behavior/

All the mice with poop from IBS sufferers developed low-grade inflammation, compared to mice colonized with bacteria from healthy individuals. The mice with anxiety-free poop continued to go about their carefree lives launching themselves dare-devil style from elevated platforms and exploring their surroundings. Meanwhile the anxiety-laden IBS poop resulted in the host mice moping in a dark corner of their cage refusing to come out and play. As if this isn't exciting enough, in another test—in which samples from healthy humans were transplanted into a family of mice—the recipients transformed from their prior state of chronic depression into a group of lovable, playful little critters behaving exactly as nature intended.

Just a word of warning—if you think this might work for you, best go talk to your GP rather than taking matters into your own hands. I suspect there are laws which discourage people loitering around public toilets in the hope of harvesting discarded poop from a happy person—regardless of whether there is a compelling medical reason to do so. Even if there isn't such a law, this is definitely a case where self-medication is best avoided.

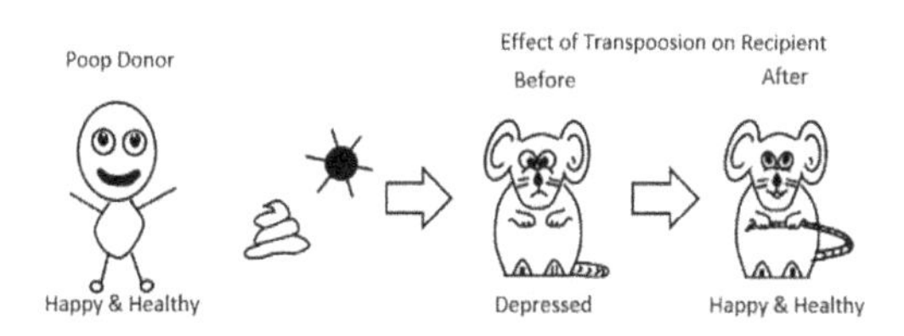

Figure 2 – Effect of Transpoosion on Depressed Mice

12

From Carnivore to Vegan

The only time I went hungry at university was when subjecting myself to yet another unsuccessful diet. Meals were often home-cooked, or alternatively sourced from a vast array of takeaways, pub lunches, or the university refectory that served up good quality and inexpensive food. And, living above a bakery meant a regular supply of cakes and bread. Except for breakfast, meat was the central ingredient of all meals. Back then, if vegetarians were catered for at all, it was only by removing the meat from a standard meal.

Bath was a truly blessed city in that it was the home of Schwartz Bros—unquestionably the best beef burgers in the entire world—just a five-minute walk from my digs. The only downside was its enormous popularity. Whatever time of day you went, it was common to spend upwards of twenty tortuous minutes drooling in anticipation, while creeping at an agonisingly slow pace towards the front of the queue. But it was *so, so* worth it.

Cheap frozen mince of dubious origin made up a large part of my emergency food rations. Being an incurably trusting person, I never gave so much as a passing thought to the content of the bag from the Bargain Buy section of the supermarket freezer. It tasted good enough when crafted into exquisite spaghetti Bolognese or chilli con carne, and washed down with copious quantities of alcohol. The journey my bag of mince took between farm and freezer was a complete mystery. Actually it's fair to say I never associated the mince with an animal that had once been alive. I had no interest in the cattle farming industry. I was not aware that cattle, which are natural herbivores, were being fed leftovers from the slaughtering process—brains, spinal cords of other cattle, in addition to carcasses of sick and injured animals such as poultry, pigs or sheep. Neither was I aware that the feed was supplemented by a delicious, growth-accelerating mélange of antibiotics, hormones, fertilizers, pesticides and protein supplements. Even if I had known of this, I suspect I would have been unconcerned. After all, I assumed anything that made it to my supermarket basket was safe to be consumed by humans.

Well, I should have been concerned. I was forced to take notice when, several years after leaving university, cattle exacted their revenge on humans in the form of Bovine Spongiform Encephalopathy, known more commonly as Mad Cow Disease. And boy did the UK population of cows have every reason to be mad. The disease was killing them in their tens of thousands by attacking the brain and spinal cord of infected animals. It also passed into the human food chain, from where it could infect anyone who ate tainted flesh. If I'd been a cow, I would have taken comfort in that.

When the issue could no longer be brushed under the carpet, the government imposed a massive eradication programme. Over 4 million cattle were destroyed by burning, and the countryside was effectively closed for business. The economic and social impact was immense. It was very much a British problem. Unlike in Europe and the US, it had become economically beneficial to feed cattle with left-over crap instead of increasingly expensive soya based feeds.

The human form of the disease was called variant Creutzfeldt-Jakob disease or vCJD for short. As with the equivalent disease in cattle, it attacked the brain, and was invariably fatal. For me, the most disturbing feature of the disease was its long incubation period. Declarations of the red top tabloids that humanity was on the brink of yet another apocalypse washed over me—I became immune to such scaremongery before I hit my teens. But serious medical establishments were busy publishing reports of sufferers whose symptoms did not appear for many years after the initial infection. This was a serious cause for concern. There was every possibility the bargain mince I had enjoyed during student life, was stuffed full of pathogens that were busily multiplying in my brain, and at any moment could kick into destructive mode. This would inevitably lead either to my rapid death. Or, far worse, my loved ones would suffer as I spent the rest of my existence in a long-term vegetative state. After a few days of worrying myself sick, I switched back to my default mode—*que sera, sera, whatever will be, will be.* I figured if I was infected, there was absolutely nothing I could do about it, and I sure as hell wasn't going to destroy whatever time I had left in a state of constant fear. I'm still here with my mental faculties reasonably intact, so hopefully I dodged that bullet. 170 citizens of the UK were not so fortunate.

Back to my student days in the early 80s. When I wanted a takeaway and Schwartz Bros was too much effort, a fried chicken chain came to the rescue. One day, I got back home with my box of tasty sustenance to discover something unchicken-like lurking under the French fries. 'Hey guys, chickens don't have long pink tails do they?' I asked my flatmates. While dangling the offending item by its unexpected appendage for all to examine. My suspicion confirmed—it was indeed a rat—do you know what I did? I took it back, politely requested that it was exchanged for a new meal, did a quick visual check to confirm the contents of the replacement box was chicken, returned home and happily tucked in. It's so hard to believe this now. I should have been grossed out and mentally scarred for life. I should have bagged the evidence, stormed into the council offices, slammed it down on the desk of a public health official, and demanded they shut the offending fast-food outlet down. NOW!!! I should have sued the wealthy chain responsible for the monstrous failing and spent the rest of my days living off a multi-million pound settlement. It's incomprehensible now why

I simply shrugged it off, filed the experience away under 'amusing stories to tell my mates/kids', and got on with my evening. WHAT THE HELL WAS WRONG WITH ME!!!

In the 1980s, meat loving carnivores dominated the world. Vegetarians were showing signs of getting a foothold with their newfangled, wacky ideas about the general badness of eating meat. Fish was possibly off their menu as well. I didn't take much notice of that growing brand of wierdos. There was an infinitely more interesting group of odd-balls popping up on local news programmes. This strange new species of human appeared to be unhealthy bags of bone who—when not swinging through the rainforest canopy gathering nuts and berries—were probably high on hallucinogenic drugs. *Magic mushrooms on a bed of wild rice anyone?* Welcome to the world of Vegans. Oh how we mocked. Fast forward three decades and these pioneering eccentrics have led the world to the brink of a Vegan Revolution. OK, so not the entire world, and maybe not a revolution, but big and exciting progress.

My journey to veganism started one day back in August 2016 when Sally said 'Mum, you've got to watch Cowspiracy. It will convince you of the need for the world to cut back drastically on animal farming, and will turn you into a vegan.' Being the obedient and obliging mother I am, I watched Cowspiracy. It did indeed have the consequences Sally predicted. I am now convinced of the urgent need for the world to break its love affair with animal farming, and I have become a vegan. (OK, except for the occasional, teeny-weeny lapses brought on by my entirely understandable desire for Galaxy milk chocolate. Yes, I know I'm weak.)

The documentary which goes by the full title of *Cowspiracy: The Sustainability Secret*, was funded through another innovation of the Millennial generation—crowdfunding. I'll dig into this amazing phenomenon later, but for now let's get back to Cowspiracy. First released in 2014, the film explores the impact of animal agriculture on the environment, and investigates the policies of major 'green' organizations on this issue. It focuses on a number of ecological concerns, including global warming, water use, deforestation, and ocean dead zones. Leonardo DiCaprio lent his popularity to the film prior to it being released on Netflix in 2015. Somewhat controversially, it suggests that animal agriculture is the primary source of environmental destruction. The film's central claim—which puts animal agriculture at the top of the eco-friendly naughty list—is disputed by some respected scientific communities, including the Union of Concerned Scientists. This group seems determined to keep fossil fuel emissions at the pinnacle of hate. Let's be honest, it's a case of 'my dad's bigger than your dad' playground taunts, and they shouldn't distract our attention from the fact that both are exceedingly ugly and dangerous threats to the future of our planet.

Cowspiracy was not the only reason I became a vegan. I happened to watch the documentary at a point in my life when I was developing a serious Ben & Jerry's habit, which was threatening to take me on an unwelcome journey back up through the BMI scale. My commitment to veganism not only made Sally happy but also meant it would be so much easier for me to give up the calorie-laden Chocolate Fudge Brownie and Cookie Dough ice cream, which was beginning to make my trousers feel tight. I had sampled non-dairy ice cream and reasoned it was so awful I wouldn't want to go near it. Or so I thought. It seems the vegan food technologists at Booja-Booja—a company based in Norfolk, UK—had been hard at work creating an amazingly good range of vegan ice cream. Fortunately though, it was expensive and local stockists were limited, so veganism did help me cut back and eventually break my ice cream habit. As of now I haven't relapsed—even though I regularly walk past Tesco freezers that are now stocked full of Ben & Jerry's new range of delicious vegan ice cream.

And so to the Vegan Revolution. Technology, in particular the ability of computers to crunch vast quantities of data, has been busy helping researchers identify the best plant combinations for optimal palatability and enhanced nutrition. For a long time it has been possible for vegans to indulge in delicious foods based on vegetables, pulses, nuts and grains. Although these foods met the needs of many, they were a poor substitute for those who demanded the same taste and texture as meat, dairy milk or eggs before they would be prepared to give up regular consumption of flesh-and-blood.

With the backing of big business, such products are lining up for another push along the vegan journey. On the fake burger front, in 2017 McDonalds ran a successful trial of vegan burgers in many of their restaurants throughout Scandinavia, and it's surely only a matter of time before McVegan burgers find their way to the US and UK customers. And then there's American start-up company Impossible Foods, whose Impossible Burger—named because of its impossibly meat-like texture—has be immensely successful in premium burger outlets in the US. At the dawn of 2018, the company had just embarked on one of the most ambitious scale-ups of any start up in the food industry, with their first large-scale factory expected to produce enough plant-based meat for *1 million Impossible Burgers every week.* That's one heck of a lot of burgers. Hopefully some will be making their way to our shores for existing and wannabe vegans who are eagerly awaiting their arrival.

I'm told many confirmed vegans aren't interested in synthetic meat products, as their taste buds have adjusted and they no longer miss the flavour. Some even claim to be repulsed by it. I am not one of them. BRING IT ON! It's not just beef alternatives that are being perfected by Impossible Foods; the company is also working hard on plant-based replicas of fish, chicken, steak, eggs and cheese. Please, please, please get on with the cheese, and add smoky bacon to the list.

Dairy milk has a long and varied list of alternatives; soy, almond, cashew, coconut, rice, oat, hemp, flax, the list goes on. Most vegans can find something to meet their needs from this selection. But there is a vocal minority who insist on an alternative that looks, tastes and can be used like real milk, and has the same (if not improved) nutrient content. Well, two bioengineers may have come to the rescue: Perumal Gandhi and Ryan Pandya—take a bow. They have spent years on a quest to develop such a product using a process they describe as akin to brewing craft beer. They ferment dairy yeast and sugar, then add plant fats, nutrients, and proteins that can be found in milk, including casein, the protein that gives milk its culinary versatility and melted cheese its delightful—and essential—oozy stretchiness. This amazing product is marketed under the name Perfect Day.

Now, for no reason other than it fits perfectly into the category of quirky facts that bring happiness and joy to mankind, I'm going to enlighten you with the origin of the name. Apparently the idea took hold after Gandhi and Pandya uncovered a study conducted in 2001 by a group of researchers from the University of Leicester. For twelve hours a day over a period of nine weeks, a herd of 1,000 Holstein Friesian cows were exposed to fast and slow music, while a control group went about their daily lives without the pleasures of any such rhythmic accompaniment. The results showed that fast music reduced their yield while slow music increased it by 3%. The easy rhythm of Lou Reed's 'Perfect Day' was one of the favourite slow tracks played throughout the 'Moosic Study'.

After experimenting briefly with vegetarianism, Sally became a full-on vegan in 2016. The fact that she had no real love for fruit or vegetables undoubtedly made her conversion much more of a challenge than if she's been happy to munch her way through the contents of the fruit bowl or a bag of carrots from the fridge. But she persevered and eventually settled on a healthy, balanced vegan diet in which she also avoids palm oil and other plant products that cause excessive damage to the environment. In the early days avocado was on the naughty list. Now she's happy to indulge occasionally, particularly if the fruit has come from Spain rather than from less environmentally sustainable areas such as South and Central America.

Sally's brand of veganism also excludes honey—a bit of a grey area and a frequent topic of heated debate. Sun-dried, crushed beetle is another product that has been struck off her menu. It's strange to think this particular delicacy was ever on anyone's menu, but it is used in red food colouring as a natural replacement for nasty, carcinogenic E-numbers.

The question whether or not to eat beetles presents quite a conundrum to health-conscious vegans who also have social responsibility high on their list of personal values. You see, natural red food colouring comes from the cochineal insect that lives almost exclusively on cacti, and is of great economic importance to the small communities in Peru, Mexico and the Canary Islands that produce it. The question Sally is grappling with is this: should vegans be encouraged to avoid the product if it will cause financial hardship to a small community? Also, there is the issue of health, as the main alternative is a cancer-inducing synthetic dye. Do you really want your own mortality and the impact on the already-over-stretched NHS troubling your mind as you're about to launch into a big wedge of gorgeous red velvet cake? Clearly the higher number of important causes you're passionate about, the more complicated life gets.

There's one often overlooked fact about veganism that I feel duty-bound to point out. I know it's a statement of the bleeding obvious, but I'll make it anyway: Veganism and Healthy ARE NOT synonymous. You can be 100% vegan by consuming a diet of nothing but tachos and sugar-laden cola. For proof you need to look no further than the increasing number of vegan junk food cafes that are springing up to profit from our craving for refined sugars and other tasty nutritional crap. Let's be clear about this: vegans do not have a natural immunity to the desire to consume food of dubious nutritional value. I recently went with Sally to Vegan Fest, which took place in a sizeable venue next to Bristol's central railway station. The £3 entry fee gave us access to row after row and stall after stall of vegan fare, which had been laid out alluringly to tempt the hundreds of eager visitors. I'm going to risk the wrath of vegans everywhere and state that hardly any of it was healthy. Attractively presented cakes, chocolates, truffles, cheese, flapjacks, ice-cream and other sugar-filled delights attacked my willing senses. All the vendors were beautiful and welcoming sirens, attracting people to their stalls by the offer of free samples of their truly heavenly products. It would have been impolite to turn down any one of them, so I dutifully tried every single thing on offer. I was so hooked on the experience, I suspect I even sampled the colourful cake-like blocks of vegan soap and cosmetics. I spent no more than three hours either side of Saturday noon enjoying the delights of the festival. As I got up for work on Monday morning, pure sugar continued to course through my veins, while my digestive system was still bitterly complaining about the effects of my vegan over-indulgence.

13

The Environment

Until recently I never worried much about the environment. Planet Earth is such an enormous place I found it difficult to believe human behaviour could possibly have any significant impact. Certainly not the kind of impact that fuelled protests from the likes of Green Peace, or the less prominent local eco-warriors who chained themselves to railings with the goal of preventing a monstrous new development from destroying their local meadow. I classified these people somewhere between harmless nutters and unwelcome barriers to economic growth. I always had a tendency to believe western governments and big businesses when they made assured declarations that fossil fuel wasn't going to run out any time soon; leaded petrol wasn't the cause of increased cases of brain damage and birth defects; aerosols weren't the reason the ozone layer was thinning out to the point of no return. The problem I had was most environmental arguments seemed to be based on emotion, backed up by flimsy evidence, and championed by dislikeable people with their own personal agenda. Back then I had no awareness of the power big business was exercising to silence whistleblowers, and to suppress the truth. It was only these unpleasant, loud, snarling people who had the strength and courage to make their voices heard.

In addition to mistrusting emotional arguments, I also avoided anything based on short-term data. Anyone who used unusual peaks in water levels, the driest summer for 200 years, or the highest

March temperature since 1825 as evidence of human-induced global warming was clearly deluded. If human behaviour was the cause, I'd want to see sustained evidence of the highest/driest <*fill in the blank*> since records began. Even then, there's every chance it was just a normal blip caused by entirely natural phenomenon such as the earth's wobbly orbit or el Niño, both of which have long-established histories of disrupting normal weather patterns. It was natural phenomena that—several thousand years ago—created large tracts of Sahara desert from what had previously been fertile land. Natural phenomena were the likely culprits behind the demise of pre-Columbian civilisations in Central and South America.

The brutal reality is we're currently enjoying a period of balmy weather before the next Ice Age kicks in. What's more, a scientific study by the Potsdam Institute for Climate Impact Research in Germany, which was widely reported in January 2016, pretty much proved that if humans hadn't started pumping carbon dioxide into the environment when we did, we'd be heading full speed into the next Ice Age. According to that report, human activity has delayed the onset of the next Ice Age by about 50,000 years. So that's a good thing right? Proves the climate warriors were just trying to whip up some good old-fashioned hysteria and didn't know what they were talking about? Well no, not really. We didn't need to delay the next ice age at all, because it's not expected for another 50,000 years. Given the current rate of technological advances, 50,000 years would have been ample time for us humans to figure out a solution without all the other bad things happening—like ice caps melting and sea levels rising. But general expert opinion is clear: if we don't drastically change our ways huge areas of land will be submerged and uninhabitable. Yes, we might kick the next Ice Age out by another 50,000 years, but it won't do us much good unless we develop gills and go back to living with the fishes.

Global warming or no global warming, it's impossible to avoid the conclusion that humans are using the planet as a garbage dump. We are destroying environments, punching a hole through the ozone layer and indulging in a whole host of other behaviours that are having a devastating impact on our planet and its inhabitants. As you've no doubt picked up by now, I am not an innately emotional person. Yet I was horrified by some of the footage from the BBC's amazing Blue Planet II series—in particular the plastic which is littering our oceans, and killing marine life in diverse and truly sickening ways. One episode followed devoted albatross parents making long and exhausting journeys to catch fish for their chicks, just to find that the food they were bringing back contained all manner of plastics that caused illness and, in some cases, death. The images of an albatross chick that had been killed by a toothpick piercing its stomach were extremely upsetting. An insignificant piece of plastic, once used to remove a tiny fragment of food from the teeth of a human, ends up thousands of miles away, where it is responsible for the death of a majestic, innocent chick. I couldn't help but feel a deep sense of guilt and regret. Maybe it was *my* toothpick—carelessly discarded on my plate at a restaurant thirty years ago—that resulted in the death of that albatross chick. But no, I don't blame myself—that would be too great a burden to carry. Instead—thanks to the magic of Google—I can point my accusing finger at the true villain. Robert B Briggs, the American inventor who in December 1952 was granted patent US2760628A for Plastic Toothpicks, which he claimed had none of the 'objectionable' features of the wooden variety. 'Objectionable' features such as splintering in the mouth of an unsuspecting user leading to painful gum infections, often followed by unpleasant tooth extraction. What a despicable, inconsiderate, money grabbing excuse for a human being Briggs must have been. The United States Patent and Trademark Office were just as guilty. They had both the opportunity and power to stop this tiny—but lethal—weapon of destruction from ever being unleashed on an unsuspecting world. BUT THEY DID NOTHING!!!!

OK. Just kidding. I don't hold Briggs or the US government responsible for the proliferation of tooth picks. Not at all. Plastic is an amazing human invention, which back in the 50s had a seemingly unlimited potential to improve lives. Plastic toothpicks packed in their own tiny, germ-free sleeve (also included in Briggs' patent) were indeed safer and considerably more hygienic than their long-established wooden rivals. When it came to plastic packaging, consumers couldn't get enough of it. Anyone over the age of 40 will surely remember flexible metal tubes of toothpaste. The packaging was memorable because of its tendency to spring a leak and squirt its thick, messy white content all over your favourite item of clothing. Frequently in a pattern that looked embarrassingly like you'd been caught in the path of bird droppings. Metal toothpaste tubes were just one of packaging disasters consigned to history by the rise of plastic. Hurrah for plastic!

In many ways plastic became a victim of its own success, and the fact the material didn't degrade was viewed as a positive feature. The problem is that no one back in the 50s (or 60s, 70s, 80s and 90s for that matter) gave much thought to what happened to the non-degradable, non-recyclable plastic mountain that would inevitably result from its ever expanding usefulness. I suspect there were people who worried deeply about such things—but they lived in underground bunkers from which they only emerged after carefully wrapping their heads in long sheets of tin foil, and survived by eating small, furry rodents captured in homemade traps. When the rest of us did give it any thought, we quickly dismissed it as SEP, otherwise known as Somebody Else's Problem.

It's not just visible items such as crisp packets and plastic bottles that are causing devastation—microbeads may be an even greater cause of pollution in our oceans. Microbeads are tiny globules of plastic that are added as exfoliates to health and beauty products, such as face scrubs, gels and toothpaste. We have been welcoming them into our bathrooms for a very long time. In fact, since they first started replacing charcoal and other natural products about fifty years ago. After completing their miniscule contribution to the overall wellbeing of their human masters, these tiny particles leave our homes through our bathroom sinks, easily pass through any water filtration system they encounter, and end up in local rivers and streams. Then onward to the oceans. It's a disturbing fact that microbeads don't like to travel alone. The reality is they are sociable little blighters who act as a magnet for toxic pollutants such as industrial chemicals and pesticides. Once gathered together, this tiny band of trouble hops on board plankton that gets ingested by marine life, where they meet up with others to continue their destructive journey in menacing gangs, with an ever increasing membership. Up they go through the food chain. Invading their unwitting hosts in such numbers that they are responsible for the deaths of dolphins, whales and other newborn mammals who rely on the polluted milk fed to them by their mothers. Eventually, many of these microbeads will return to our homes. This time they won't be helpful individuals in a tube of gunk that keeps our teeth sparkling white and cavity-free. No, this time they'll be potent groups of nastiness hidden in full view on our dinner plates, in the form of fresh haddock, tinned tuna or any other flesh that was once enjoying a carefree aquatic lifestyle. Nastiness that may accumulate in our own cells, leading to illness and disease. I don't know for sure, but I suspect that it's not just fish that's a cause for concern. Everything we consume relies on water. Everything. Fish-eaters may be at greatest risk, but meat-eaters and even vegans have little room for complacency. Thankfully, since the issue became evident in 2012, many major brands have been voluntarily removing microbeads from their products, and governments are also taking positive action. In the UK for example, January 2018 saw the introduction of a ban on the manufacture of products containing microbeads, with a ban on sales following shortly afterwards.

There were many aspects of Blue Planet II that struck a chord with me. The human endeavour and technological advances that brought the most stunning footage imaginable to our screens was just part of the story. What I found encouraging was that despite numerous deeply disturbing images, the tone of the series was overwhelmingly positive. Sir David Attenborough's closing speech undoubtedly played a part in ramming home the message that all is not lost—YET. This much-loved elder statesman delivered wa powerful rallying call urging everyone to do more to protect the environment. 'Never before have we had such an awareness of what we are doing to the planet. And never before have we had the power to do something about that.' He said in his usual calm, authoritative manner, before adding 'The future of humanity, and indeed all life on earth, now depends on us.' No pressure.

While the BBC and Sir David were busy bringing the full glory of the oceans into our living rooms, and raising awareness of the urgent need for global action to prevent the problem of plastic getting worse, Boyan Slat, a remarkable young Dutch engineer, was focused on how to remove the mountain of plastic that is already out there. Slat was born in the Netherlands to Croatian immigrants in 1994. A keen diver, he was troubled by the volume of plastic he continually encountered—often coming across more items of plastic than of fish. Rather than accepting conventional wisdom that declared clean-up was impossible, Slat took the unusual step of committing to do something about it. In October 2012, while still just 18 years old, he gave a TEDx talk in his home city of Delft, during which he launched his idea to clean up five large, heavily polluted areas of the oceans. Shortly afterwards he founded a non-profit organisation—The Ocean Cleanup—with a mission to develop advanced technologies to rid the world's oceans of plastic. He then set about raising $2.2 million through a crowdfunding campaign—a target that was quickly reached with the help of 38,000 donors from across the globe. As of early 2018 he has raised in excess of $31 million in donations, and has more than 70 staff working to bring his dream to reality. Before I get into how this exceptional young man and his army of supporters plan to go about cleaning up the oceans, I'd like to give you an idea of the size of the task they are facing.

The existence of unusually high concentrations of pollution in an area of the North Pacific Ocean—roughly between Hawaii and California—was discovered in the mid to late 80s. Analysis of the area—dubbed the Great Pacific Garbage Patch—found that the pollution consisted of a massive collection of plastic, chemical sludge and other debris which had been trapped by the natural currents. Since its discovery, pollution levels have been rapidly rising due to the combined effects of the non-degradable nature of the debris and the circulating currents which are adept at sucking in—and permanently trapping— any ocean waste that passes their way. The size of the patch is hard to estimate, but is often quoted as being somewhere between the size of Texas and Russia. Add to this the fact that the North Pacific is just one of five significant oceanic garbage patches (the others being found in the South Pacific, North Atlantic, South Atlantic and Indian Oceans), and there can be no escaping the conclusion that we've created a vast monster of heavily polluted ocean.

Slat's idea was this: hc would build a passive system that used surface currents to bring debris to specially designed floating booms and collection platforms. Plankton and other naturally occurring food sources would be separated from the harmful material and returned to the ocean, while the contaminants would be taken back to land for recycling or safe disposal. He estimated that each garbage patch would take about 5 years to clean up, taking an estimated 7.25 million tons of pollutants—the weight of 1,000 Eiffel Towers—out of the oceans.

Want to find out how an 18-year-old plans to clean up the oceans?

Thankfully the team has not been deterred by technical setbacks or the occasional naysayer, and after several years of iterative improvements to the design, they expect to launch the first clean-up system in mid-2018. Following this they aim to reach full-scale deployment in the Great Pacific Garbage Patch in 2020, by which time Boyan Slat, CEO and all-round amazing Millennial, will have reached the grand old age of 26. What next for Boyan? President of the World by 30? I promise he'll get my vote.

14

Domestic Chaos

After completing a year living and working in Cambridge, Harriet was happy to return to Bristol where she was planning to continue her career in fundraising. She had used her network of contacts and her natural communication skills to set up lunch dates with top decision makers at local universities, and was positive about the future. Before starting her 'proper adult life' she wanted one last blitz of travelling. A fortnight in Bali was followed by a 3 month tour covering Australia, New Zealand, Fiji and South America. While away she applied for the fund raising job she was hoping to get. I reviewed her application and realised she is far more amazing than I had ever imagined. Life was peachy.

As I mentioned in the first paragraph of this book, she Skyped us from Fiji on Christmas Day 2017. I'd never seen her happier. She was with friends enjoying the most stunning surroundings the world has to offer. The sun was shining, and she was free to do whatever she wanted. Then I picked up a familiar sign of tension in her voice. Iånstinct told me something bad was on the way, and so it turned out. In between uncontrollable sobs, it all came pouring out. 'Mum, I can't face spending the rest of my life working in an office. I want to take another year out to find myself, and to explore my creative side. Is it OK?' The outcome was we agreed that her next 12 months would look something like...woodcarving course, painting, sewing, community projects, working in bars/cafes, and touring the music festival scene to sell her own homemade lemon drizzle cake. Plans to help her buy a flat were shelved for the time being, and she would move back home.

Now, as much as I was thrilled to welcome her home, there was a problem—a mismatch between her need for tidiness and the reality of our very untidy existence. Unable to express herself verbally, she wrote a long letter detailing how the general state of constant untidiness in our house affected her mental health. She wanted to cook and entertain her friends without having to spend hours tidying up beforehand. Being unable to do this was making her depressed. Interestingly these are the same friends who, during their teenage years, were constant and welcome visitors to our house. They came in droves for sleep overs, parties and just to slob out. Unlike in their own homes, they didn't have to worry about taking off their shoes, or leaving a plate full of uneaten pizza crust on the floor. Our untidiness was an attraction back then. It appears they've all grown up.

In our defence, we live busy lives, and tidiness has never been high up our list of priorities. Sally and I are untidy, but David is a nightmare. He has so much stuff. Sports-related stuff...gadgets... computer stuff...shoes. Boy does he have a lot of shoes. Long ago I imposed a rule that if he bought a new pair of shoes he had to throw an old pair out. OK, so let me explain that David is not a male version of Imelda Marcos with a fixation on creations from the Louis Vuitton or Gucci collections. Believe me I'm grateful for that. Instead his shoe habit provides a steady stream of revenue to brands such as Carlton and Forza. As a regular badminton and squash player he is constantly throwing himself around courts, destroying sports shoes at an alarming rate.

David's sports bags litter our hallway. Archery, badminton, squash bags and associated equipment and sweaty clothes are everywhere. We have more laundry baskets than floor space, and they're usually full of David's clothes. It's not always clear whether they're full of clean or dirty items, and quite often it's both. Clean clothes get put in a laundry basket before they embark on the tortuous trip upstairs, destination wardrobe. More often than not it's an incomplete journey, and clean clothes only get removed from the laundry basket when they're about to be used. This is not a problem until dirty items get put on top of clean ones. Countless times I've found myself throwing stuff in the washing machine that I'm certain hasn't been used since the last time I took it out. If he runs out of clean clothes, he has an annoying habit of buying new ones rather than washing the ones he already owns. Basically, my husband and his laundry process are both in desperate need of radical reform.

Our kitchen storage and stock-taking processes also appear to be sub-optimal. Harriet would like us to do things such as put tubs of margarine back in the cupboard after use. Not an unreasonable request. It should only take a couple of seconds, and job done. But here's the problem. All of our food cupboards are full to overflowing, and the mere act of removing the margarine tub starts a chain reaction that results in half-empty bottles of burger relish and mayonnaise cascading out onto the work surface, before crashing to the floor. So once we've managed to extract the margarine and slam the door shut, we're obviously reluctant to open it again. As a result, margarine and other items that are in regular use tend to stay on work surfaces rather than in cupboards.

The root of this particular problem is we accumulate. A typical scenario is we'll buy several assorted bottles of burger relish once a year for Harriet's birthday BBQ. Each one will be opened, and some will be more popular than others. Invariably there will be a reasonable quantity left in all of them, and they will be put back in the cupboard where they won't be used again until the next BBQ. By this time they'll be well out of date, so we'll throw them away and get a new set. We are most definitely creatures of habit. The same is true for many items of food that we buy; we'll use it once, stash it away for future use then forget about it until the cupboard situation gets intolerable, and I embark on a draconian clear out. In the course of these infrequent blitzes, it's not unknown for me to discover tins of food or packets of spices that passed their 'Best Before' date sometime before the dawn of the new millennium. And then there's another kitchen-related problem. Dirty dishes, pots and pans, cutlery and all sorts of other utensils accumulate in the sink and over the work surfaces, because emptying the dishwasher struggles to make it to the top of anyone's to-do list.

Generally, I accept the domestic mess as an unavoidable consequence of our busy, productive and enjoyable life style. Occasionally the mess causes something to break or spill, and will trigger me into a minor strop. But a few choice swear words later and I'm over it. I'm happy about this. Life's too short to spend any significant percentage of it doing tedious activities such as housework. Now we were faced with continuing as-is, fully aware of the impact it was having on Harriet, or change a habit of a lifetime. No contest. We simply had to change. Within minutes of making the decision—and as proof of our commitment to the cause—six assorted bottles of last summer's BBQ relish were emptied, and the bottles consigned to the recycling bin; even though they were well within their use-by date. By the end of January, new kitchen units had been installed and a host of other improvements set into motion. It won't be easy to change, but if it results in a happy daughter and the return of her wonderful friends to our home, I'm sure we'll find a way.

Update#1: It's now Easter weekend, and I think this chapter would benefit from an update. The good news is that the state of affairs with our kitchen cupboards is now under control; a clear out, new kitchen units, and the occasional nagging reminder was all it took. The bad news is that the kitchen hasn't been used for its designated purpose since the dishes were cleared up after our Christmas dinner. Since then it's been re-purposed as a workshop where David and Harriet have been busy getting to grips with an impressive array of dangerous-looking power tools for cutting, drilling and sanding wood. The kitchen surfaces are constantly covered in a thick layer of dust, while more often than not the floor is ankle-deep in wood shavings. The noise and dust got so disruptive that Heather, our tortoise, begged to go back into hibernation until the weather was warm enough for her to go out in the garden. But that would have been bad for her health, so instead we let her wander around the living room for a few months. Much to the chagrin of Rupert, our long-suffering dog, Heather soon mastered the art of plonking herself between him and the fire. Rupert, showing his true colours as the world's biggest wuss, simply accepted his position at the bottom of the family hierarchy, and would get up and trudge crestfallen to his bed in the corner, where he would indulge himself in a good cry at the injustice of life.

Update#2: It's now the end of May and I've nearly finished the writing phase for this book. So unless something truly spectacular happens in the next few months, this will be the last update. The workshop has been relocated to our garden shed, and our kitchen has finally been reclaimed. David and I celebrated this milestone by sitting down at the kitchen table to enjoy a meal for the first time since Christmas Day. Heather is outside enjoying the British sunshine, and Rupert has his place back in front of the gas fire. Unfortunately we are no longer allowed to turn the fire on. An engineer who came to fit a Smart Meter identified it was leaking gas, promptly turned off the supply and adorned the offending item with a large and brightly coloured sticker with the words 'DANGER. SAFETY WARNING. DO NOT USE'. It's one thing after another in old houses. Really it is. If it's not the kitchen ceiling collapsing because of a leaking radiator in the room above, it's the electrics blowing because of water leaking through a hole in the bath (which incidentally was made by my head when I slipped getting out of the shower to open the door to a delivery driver). Or it is water steadily dripping in through the loft as a massive snowdrift on the roof carefully directs its melt water through a strategically placed airbrick. Yes, one thing after another. I suppose we should be grateful for the discovery of the gas leak, because it now forces us to strip out the hideous old contraption (which was hideous and old when we bought the house back in 1986). But more importantly, the discovery might just have saved us and our neighbours from a gas explosion which rips out the entire terrace of Victorian houses, destroying our new kitchen units in the process. I'm sure we'll get around to fixing it one day, but for now our focus has shifted to sorting out the continuing disaster that is our—no DAVID's—laundry problem.

15

The Language of Love

The hardest part of writing this chapter has been finding the appropriate words. During my first five decades on this planet, I haven't been aware of much development in the English language beyond the widespread acceptance of Ms. as an alternative to Mrs or Miss. Gay and Lesbian have finally moved beyond playground insults, and entered common, acceptable usage—but how should these words be used without causing offence? Are they, for example, adjectives used to describe a person, as in a gay man and a lesbian woman, or is it also acceptable to use them on their own as a noun—a gay, or a lesbian? Then there's an ever increasing list that includes Transsexual, Transgender, Bisexual, Pansexual, Asexual, A-romantic, Polyamorous, Non-binary, Gender-fluid, Queer, Questioning...the list goes on. It is a list that has become so long the LGBT community now often uses LGBT+, instead of constantly dealing with the hassle of adding a string of new letters to the end.

Do people even want a label? A recent advertising campaign for a popular brand of alcoholic drink led me to believe that labels are for bottles—not people. Another question. Does this group of words fall under the banner of sexual orientations, sexual persuasions, life styles or is there another more appropriate term I've missed? And what about combinations of words? I now know polyamorous can be used in combination with at least some of the other terms, but what about asexual? Is it possible, for example, to be an asexual transsexual? Theoretically it should be—as it would describe someone who lacked interest in sex and also identified their gender differently from their assigned sex. And what about transgender? Is there such a thing as a transgender man, and if so is it someone born a man who identifies as a woman, the reverse of this or do both definitions apply?

Wow. So many questions. I've clearly got a lot of learning to do before I can communicate effectively in the language of love. Sure, I could turn to the Oxford English Dictionary for approved definitions, but I'd rather go with real world usage. Sally, with input from her assortment of gender non-conformist friends, has agreed to provide me with a crash course. So, here goes. If my choice of language is inappropriate, please accept that I mean no offence.

Back in 'the olden days' options were limited and, at least in my circle of the known world, life was simple. Boy met girl, fell in love, got married and had kids. Usually, but not exclusively, in that order. Occasionally the boy and girl fell out of love and got divorced, with varying degrees of devastation on their own lives and the lives of their children. Anyone who didn't fit the mould either stayed silent, lived a lie or—if they chose to live as openly gay or lesbian—endured a regular dose of discrimination and abuse from a largely bigoted and intolerant society. Whichever of the limited alternatives they chose, the chances are they lived miserable and unfulfilled lives.

Had these same gay men lived in or before Roman times, life may have been much kinder to them. In fact if they'd been living in the higher echelons of society during the time of the great philosophers of Ancient Greece, they would have been encouraged—indeed expected—to engage in homosexual behaviour. Pederasty, a romantic relationship between an adult and an adolescent male, was a perfectly normal practice back then. So normal that the Sacred Band of Thebes—an elite force of the Theban army in the 4th century BC—was formed from 150 pairs of male lovers, each pair consisting of an adult and adolescent. In addition, many of the famous names from antiquity were openly homosexual. For example Alexander the Great—widely acknowledged as one of the greatest military leaders of all time—had a male lover.

It wasn't until Christian and Muslim religions took hold that the anti-gay sentiment found in the Old Testament began to impose a new set of norms in the societies over which they had control. However, outside the area of influence of these religions, for example in South East Asia where Buddhism held sway, organised repression of non-heterosexual behaviour never really occurred. These societies remain largely accepting of the idea that gender exists on a continuous spectrum rather than being a simple binary state.

The intolerant view of Christianity was the foundation for my parents' generation, and remained dominant throughout the formative years of Baby Boomers and Gen Xers. Not that I knew any lesbians or gays personally. Of course I knew of the existence of gay men. AIDs was rampant during my 20s, and headlines declaring it was '*God's punishment for gays*' were hard to avoid. As was the desperately sad decline and death of Freddie Mercury that deprived the world of a musical genius. I was in my 30s before I met an openly gay man in real life, and another few years before I could call a gay couple among my friends. Then later still came my first confirmed lesbian—one of my own nieces.

Gradually, as my young relatives grew up, I became aware of a clear trend away from standard heterosexual behaviours. Of my 3 nieces and nephews in their late twenties to early thirties who are in committed relationships (by which I mean married or engaged) only one is in a conventional heterosexual arrangement. Of the others, there is one gay man engaged to his long-term partner, and one lesbian who has a child resulting from artificial insemination, as well as having two step-daughters from her wife who was previously married to a man. Together they make a wonderful, loving family.

I recently got to know another non-heterosexual Millennial through two students who were doing some dog walking work for me, let's call them Janet and John. Based on appearances, Janet was female, and John male. One day Janet got injured, and I went to her house to check on her. 'How's Janet?' I ask John. 'Oh, he's broken his toe, but he'll be back on his feet in a couple of weeks.' John replied. Certain I'd heard correctly, but not entirely sure what it meant, I returned home to consult the Oracle on such matters. 'Hey Sally', I ask, 'John referred to Janet as "he". What's that all about?' To which Sally filled me in on how transgender people often use the pronoun of the gender they identify with, rather than that of their assigned sex. Although I'd read plenty about transgender people, Janet was the first I'd met. It took me until my mid-50s.

In the few months since I started writing this book I have had conversations about the subject with many colleagues and friends who occupy the 45+ age group, and a consistent picture has emerged about their 15 to mid-30s offspring and friends. A surprisingly large number of them do not identify fully with the gender assigned to them at birth. More noticeable though are the number who are entirely supportive of—and often have personal experience of—non-heterosexual relationships. Take Sally for example. One Sunday during lunch she casually drops into the conversation, 'Mum, I think I should tell you I'm bi-sexual'. This came as a complete surprise, considering she recently moved in with her boyfriend of more than 2 years. 'OK. No problem. I'm glad you told me', I replied thinking it changes nothing—she was in a relationship with a man now, if they ever broke up her next relationship could be with either a man or a woman. I'm cool with that. It was when she then threw in 'I'm also polyamorous' that I felt by brain beginning to hurt.

Wikipedia provides the following definition: *Polyamory is the practice of, or desire for, intimate relationships with more than one partner, with the knowledge of all partners. It has been described as "consensual, ethical, and responsible non-monogamy".*

OK, now I'm getting confused. 'So what does your boyfriend think of this?' Apparently 'he's struggling'.

I suppose the basis of polyamory is common throughout pre-Millennial generations, but back then it was more like '*non-consensual, unethical, and irresponsible non-monogamy'.* Anyone involved in the practice was simply referred to as being *'a cheating bastard'.* I guess even in the modern world, polyamorous Millennials are far outnumbered by those of their generation who fit into the latter description.

Of all the different orientations I have come across, gender-fluid is the one I find most difficult to comprehend. The hyphenated word gained full recognition in the English language back in 2016 when, along with *moobs* and *yolo*, it found its way into the Oxford English dictionary. Moobs—as I'm sure you already know—is just another word for man-boobs, while yolo is the acronym for the phrase *'you only live once'*. I've long been familiar with (and a regular user of) both moobs and yolo, but gender-fluid has only recently been introduced to my vocabulary. I now know it is used to describe a person who does not identify with a single fixed gender. However, *knowing* what the term means, is not the same as *understanding* what it means. Turning to the Urban Dictionary for more information, I find the following slightly more expansive description:

> *An individual who is genderfluid experiences their sense of gender identity shift around the spectrum. They may feel like a boy one day, a girl another, or neutral, or everything at once, or nothing, or something different entirely. This is a completely normal gender identity; being genderfluid is not a mental illness. Gender has nothing do with genitals.*

I have to admit that I struggle with the assertion, *'This is a completely normal gender identity'.* Is it really? Maybe this is just another example of the Urban Dictionary's lower standard of English than the good 'ole equivalent from Oxford. If what they mean is *'completely acceptable', or 'completely natural'*, fine. I'd agree 100% with that. *But 'completely normal'?* I don't think so. Maybe I'm wrong, maybe it is completely normal, and it's just that not a single person I know has ever admitted to being gender-fluid. Regardless of how many people now associate with the term, what I find of great interest is whether gender-fluidity is a modern phenomenon as well as a modern term. Was the feeling experienced (albeit not acknowledged) by as many Silents, Boomers and Gen Xs as it is by Millennials? That is a question that not even Google can throw any light on, so I will carry out my own research through the magic of an online blog at www.motherofmillennials.co.uk. If you'd like to get involved at the cutting-edge of research, please feel free to visit and complete a questionnaire. It asks for nothing more than the year of your birth, your assigned sex at birth, current sex, current gender and whether you have ever considered yourself to be gender-fluid.

Throughout this chapter I have highlighted my lack of understanding of how to use the available vocabulary appropriately, and without causing offense. However, I can't help but notice a glaring inadequacy in the area of suitable pronouns. *He* and *She* are simply no longer sufficient as a growing number of people associate with neither—or both. *They* hasn't caught on as a singular pronoun, and *it* is considered by most as degrading. I get annoyed when David, my dear husband, refers to my dog as an 'it'—I doubt I would be comfortable using the pronoun for a human, even if that is what *it* wanted. Dear LGBT+ community, I would like to ask you a question. Please accept it comes from a place of ignorance, and I mean no offence by it… WHAT IS WRONG WITH YOU PEOPLE???? You've overcome so much pain, suffering and discrimination. You've broken taboos. You've won the general acceptance of the western world to live and love as you choose. And yet you continue to muddle through life with outdated, hand-me-down vocabulary. Surely the time is right to rise up and fight for your right for a pronoun. Join forces with the movers and shakers of the English language, and demand a brand new set of three related words created by you, for you. Discard forever he/him/his, she/her/hers and the appalling gender neutral and plural alternatives. How hard can it be to create 3 tiny words and sneak them in to the English language? The king of Swaziland might be a good source of advice, after all he has just created a brand new name for his entire country—eSwatini. Alternatively, you might look to brand owners of vegan and vegetarian foods for inspiration. As a result of new laws in France—and likely to follow elsewhere—the world's leading marketing companies are frantically banging their linguistic heads together to create new words for sausages, steaks, cheese, milk and other foods historically associated with animals. Be brave. Be bold. Break the rules. Remember, it is not written in law that 'i' has to come before 'e', except after 'c'. Neither is it a criminal offense to follow the letter 'q' by something other than 'u'.

If I were the all-powerful master of the English language, and could impose my choice of words, I would choose qes, qeo, qep—pronounced 'kes', 'keeyo' and 'kep'—for reasons I will now explain. When I consulted the Pride News acronym guide, I was truly astonished to find that 'queer' is no longer considered a derogatory insult, but has instead been adopted as an umbrella term freely available for use by any non-heterosexual. At station Q of the alphabet you'll also find the word used by individuals who are exploring their gender identity and/or sexual orientation. In homage to questioners and queers, I have chosen 'q' as the initial letter in my pronouns. I would suggest it is pronounced as 'k' in 'kick', or indeed the 'Q' in Qatar, a country in the Middle East where homosexuality is illegal and punishable by imprisonment. As an aside. If you have even a passing interest in football, you are likely to know that Qatar will host the 2022 FIFA World Cup. What you perhaps don't know is that in that Richard de Mos, a member of the Dutch Parliament for the Freedom Party, proposed that the Dutch football team play in pink instead of their normal orange kit to protest at Qatar's stance on gay rights. Just a thought, but after Holland's unexpected failure to qualify for the 2018 finals, it might be better if next time around the players focus their attention on the quality of their football, rather than worrying about what shade of pink will suit them best. Anyway, returning to my new non-specific gender pronouns. I have chosen 'e' as the second letter because it bears a passing resemblance to the yin and yang symbol. This felt suitable as it depicts the complementary, interconnected and interdependent nature of seemingly contrary forces. The final letter was selected for the purely practical reason of indicating the form of a pronoun. This gives us 's' for the subject of a sentence, 'o' for the object and 'p' for the possessive form. So, for what it's worth, there's my suggestion for a gender-neutral world. 'He gave him a kiss' would become 'Qes gave qeo a kiss'. While 'She married his sister' would be translated as 'Qes married qep sister'. I know it sounds strange, and I certainly wouldn't be offended if others were to propose more elegant and appropriate alternatives. All I ask of the LGBT+ community is you take positive action to improve the pronoun situation. Whatever you choose will feel unnatural at first, but as you know all too well, change takes time and is always accompanied by some measure of discomfort.

16

Generational Stereotypes

Much has been written about the Millennial generation, and how their values and circumstances differ from those generations that came before them. Now, I promise I will not quote a single statistic in this chapter. Most of my views are derived from my own life experiences, and what my two Millennial daughters and their friends have told me. I have also stated a few generally accepted 'facts', and have called on one trusted and influential study—The Deloitte Millennial Survey 2017. This study involved nearly 8,000 Millennials from across 30 countries, most of whom have college or university degrees, and are working full-time predominantly in large, private-sector organisations. Although this is only a small subset of Millennials, they are important because it is this group that is increasingly taking on senior positions in the most influential businesses across the globe.

BORING! Still here? Thanks for hanging on. I'll admit that last paragraph was a rather dull introduction and I'm in real danger of abandoning this chapter. Remember my 80:20 approach I told you about earlier? I think this might be a good time to write a few glib bullet points and move on to something less difficult. But I won't. I'm not a quitter. Instead I will take a very deep breath and face up to the subject I'm reluctant to write about. So before I get into the much happier world of Millennials, and how they're attempting to save humanity, I will first review the culture that permeated leading global organisations and institutions while previous generations—the Silent Generation, Baby Boomers and my own Generation X—have been at the helm. I'll warn you now, it's depressing.

Let's start with the horrific and sustained child abuse—and subsequent determined cover-ups—carried out by members of the Roman Catholic Church, politicians and celebrities. Crimes which had been going on for decades, but only grabbed serious media attention following the death of Jimmy Savile in 2012. One case would have been bad enough, but Savile's death opened the floodgates. The sustained abuse committed by celebrities and people in positions of power and trust was brutally exposed. Stuart Hall, Rolf Harris and Gary Glitter were among many paedophiles to be convicted and imprisoned. All of these were people who had been on my childhood list of favourite entertainers.

Then there was the extensive exploitation of child labour and poorly paid adults, who produced cheap clothing for global retailers to sell on to consumers in the affluent west. In China, Bangladesh and many other countries, children as young as 10 years old routinely worked 60 hours or more a week for just a few dollars. It took the 2013 collapse of the Rana Plaza building in Bangladesh, to drive home to western consumers the dangerous conditions that producers of many of our top branded clothes were forced to work in. Over eleven hundred young Bangladeshi workers died, and thousands more were seriously injured in the name of cheap fashion.

Another low-light of the pre-Millennial organisational culture was the corporate greed and corruption that led to the collapse of many mega corporations, along with the imprisonment of a significant number of their senior executives and employees. Long-established businesses such as Enron, Worldcom, Poly Peck, Bernard Madoff and Barings Bank all fell, either because of the direct criminal behaviour or the unbelievable negligence of those in charge. Powerful tobacco companies continued to enjoy the support and protection of politicians, long after overwhelming scientific evidence had been presented that proved their products caused cancer. Major Banks and other financial institutions increased their profits by deliberately selling inappropriate products to their loyal, trusting customers.

There's plenty more I could write about, but I think that should be enough to get across the message that pre-Millennial generations have been in charge while lots of appalling shit has happened.

Now, while there can be little argument that pre-Millennial generations are entirely to blame for the woes of the past, I'm not going to suggest that the same generations have made no efforts to improve. This would be a disservice to many individuals and groups from earlier generations who have challenged the norm and set the foundations for change. People like the non-aggressive 'tree-hugging wierdos' I maligned in my early twenties. People like brothers Rob and Paul Harrison, who along with Jane Turner founded Ethical Consumer, a magazine that was first published in 1989 and continues to provide a platform for helping consumers make ethical choices. It also co-ordinates boycotts against organisations who are behaving in unethical ways. People like Juliet Gellatley, the founder of Viva!—a charity which promotes veganism and organises campaigns against animal cruelty. Until I started writing this chapter, I had no idea that Viva! is based less than 2 miles from my home in Bristol. I only discovered this when I followed an intriguing link on the Ethical Consumer website to a campaign being run by Viva! that was calling for the boycott of Adidas against their use of kangaroo leather in football boots. Who'd have thought it? A campaign against the use of kangaroo leather in football boots, being championed by a charity based just down the road from me in Bristol City Centre, on the other side of the world from where the kangaroos were being slaughtered. Interestingly, I had just finished binge watching the first two series of *Dirk Gently Holistic Detective Agency* on Netflix, and it's difficult to disagree with Mr Gently—all things in the universe are indeed connected.

Many of the high-profile scandals served as a wakeup call to pre-Millennial generations. With or without the input of Millennials, it's inconceivable that people in power will continue to abuse children on the industrial scale of the past. Potential offenders now know there is a high probability that either their victims or whistle blowers will speak out. They know that use of the dark web and bitcoin no longer guarantee they'll be able to cover up their crimes. And when they're convicted, they know they will spend many years of their pathetic lives in prison. They also know that prisons are a particularly bad place to be if you're a convicted paedophile. On the corporate front, regulations and auditing standards have been tightened so that company executives can't cook the books with the same ease as in the past. Significant jail terms are an added incentive for them to act inside the law.

I firmly believe that the values and skills Millennials have brought to the table are now accelerating the pace of change towards a fairer, kinder and more tolerant society. So just what are these skills and values I speak of? And just what can we expect the lazy, narcissistic, entitled, Me Me Me generation to do for us?

Well, let's start with tolerance and diversity. I've already written about how Millennials are far more aware and accepting of the full spectrum of non-heterosexual orientations than preceding generations, so I won't cover that again. But what about gender equality in the workplace and leading institutions? How do modern attitudes differ from previous generations in this area? Well, the life and times of Barbie Millicent Roberts provides an ideal lens through which to examine this important question.

Better known to the world by her first name, Mattel's forever-young icon celebrates her 60th birthday on 9th March 2019. Barbie was created by Ruth Handler—inventor, wife, mother and co-founder of Mattel—in response to watching her own daughter spend endless hours acting out childhood fantasies with homemade paper dolls. In the words of Handler, *"My whole philosophy of Barbie was that, through the doll, the little girl could be anything she wanted to be. Barbie always represented the fact that a woman has choices."* In the early days Handler's assumption must have been that girls wanted nothing more than to be leading ladies in blockbuster Hollywood films, as the first dolls to hit a somewhat sceptical market mimicked the glamour of 1950s stars such as Elizabeth Taylor and Marilyn Monroe. But she stayed true to her philosophy, and throughout the 60s and 70s as I was growing up Barbie was busy expanding her experience and climbing the career ladder. In 1961 she started work as a registered nurse, but before long was hopelessly stressed out due to the long hours, poor pay and complete lack of respect shown to her by the male doctors. After embarking on a quarter life crisis, she found her new calling as an astronaut. That was one hell of a career change. Good on you girl! While conspiracy theorists still throw scorn on Neil Armstrong's claim to be the first *man* on the moon, there's no questioning that Barbie became the first *woman* on the moon four years earlier in 1965. On her return to earth, her new-found fame and fortune enabled her to take a prolonged career break, move to Malibu and spend much of her time relaxing on the beach, while snogging her tanned hunk of a boyfriend, Ken. Eventually tiring of this shallow, hedonistic lifestyle, she retrained as a surgeon and Olympic athlete, before once again finding the meaningful employment and work-life balance she so craved.

As a football-playing tomboy, Barbie had no place in my young life. Even if I'd been aware of her high-flying career (which I wasn't), I doubt she would have had much of an influence on my future direction. Her message seemed to be that girls could achieve anything they wanted in life—as long as they were endowed with long, slender legs, surgically enhanced boobs, skinny waist and the ability to pursue their goals in life while staying upright on impossibly high-heeled shoes. Sadly I laid claim to none of these attributes.

Boomer and Gen X mums led the way in demanding greater career diversity to inspire our Millennial daughters. In the ten-year period starting in1985, and having invested in a wide range of sensible footwear, Barbie's career adventures resumed as she became a veterinary surgeon and a pilot, before enrolling with both the police and firefighter services. But despite her obvious talents, Barbie was unable to force her way into boardrooms, and she also failed miserably in several attempts at running for President of the USA. It appeared that—like many highly successful and talented real life women—she just wasn't taken seriously for these powerful, high-profile roles. It's no wonder she slipped into a prolonged period of depression and her fortunes went into decline for many years.

Meanwhile back in the real world, career opportunities for women had expanded. By the late 20th century many women had matched the achievements of Barbie. One such success was Helen Sharman who beat 13,000 rivals (I don't have the stats, but I suspect they were mostly men) for the honour of becoming Britain's first astronaut in 1991. A number of women even went far beyond what Barbie had achieved, but they were few and far between. In the political arena for example, Margret Thatcher became Britain's first female Prime Minister in 1979, a position she made her own for over a decade. In 1994 the Church of England ordained Angela Berners-Wilson as their first female priest. The dawn of a new millennium saw further progress when Clara Furse became the first woman to be appointed chief executive of the London Stock Exchange, and a few years later the appointment of Patricia Scotland to the role of Attorney General was hailed as a historic breakthrough, both for women and ethnic minorities. I've no reason to doubt these women were fully deserving of their positions, but I suspect positive discrimination also played a role in enabling some women to get less deserved promotions, ahead of their more able or more experienced male counterparts. On a personal level, I'm pretty certain that in 1978 there was at least one talented 17-year-old male who missed out on a lucrative engineering sponsorship with Rolls Royce, as a direct result of the organisation having to meet a pre-defined quota for female undergraduates. That must have really sucked for him.

As the first of the Millennials grew up and embarked on their own parenting journey, the number of white women being promoted to senior positions was growing, while the trail-blazing

Barbie struggled against depression, as she failed to find the love and respect of this new generation of parents. Their real-world focus had shifted from the battle for sexual equality, to the now more pressing concerns of improving the body image of young girls, and also making a step change towards racial equality. Constant body-shaming, and claims of racial isolationism and narcissism, had been significant contributors to Barbie's decline. Desperate to regain the admiration she had enjoyed in the past, Mattel knew they had to evolve Barbie in both mind and body, and to make her more relevant to the values this new generation of parents wanted to pass on to their own children. In spring 2016, their response was admirable as they re-invented their troubled daughter to be more representative of the modern world. They released a new range of Barbie with seven skin tones, and three new body shapes—tall, curvy and petite—were added to the original. Since then the range has been extended even further with Barbie taking on the likeness of over 30 inspirational women. For example, in November 2017, the first hijab-wearing Barbie doll was released to honour the American medal-winning fencer Ibtihaj Muhammad, who became the first US woman to wear the Islamic headscarf while competing at the Olympics. As I sit writing this book Nicola Adams, the beautiful, black, British boxer, and two times Olympic gold medallist, has just been added to the range. Barbie is back. Time to let the LGBT+ community get stuck into her next evolution?

Don't get me wrong, I'm not saying that the mix of men and women in senior positions is reflective of society in general. It's not, but the trend is clearly in the right direction, and there's no going back. In today's world Millennials expect to see diversity in board level and senior management roles. I've been told by my legions of Millennial friends that any organisation that is run primarily by middle aged white men is a big turn-off to them, both as a place of work and as a company they're willing to spend their money with. Let's see how this ties with reality by looking at their top 2 favourite companies as identified by advertising agency Moosylvania, who analysed 15,000 responses from Millennials.

Top of the chart is Apple. Millennials are long-term fans of Apple's iPhones, iPads, MacBooks and Apple Watches. It's not just the products they love, they are also genuinely excited by the company's vision and purpose. As of today, the senior leadership team at Apple is made up of 11 men and 5 women. Judging by their photos I'd say they're all Caucasians.

In second place is Nike who have evolved from just selling traditional sports clothing to mastery of the athleisure wear market. Athleisure is a fashion trend that feeds off Millennials' preference for experiences rather than material things. From SoulCycle to CrossFit boxes to the popularity of Tough Mudders, young people are spending more money on fitness, and in order to participate effectively they must look and feel good. Nike lists nine top executives—7 men and 2 women. All except 1 black man, appear white. Together the mix of the 25 top executives from these two organisations strongly supports the view that sexual inequality is on the wane, but racial inequality remains entrenched.

So Millennials win hands down in tolerance and diversity. What about social, economic and environmental concerns? Well, it would also be hard to argue against their superiority in these areas. In the past, many successful businesses believed the only reason for their existence was to maximize return on investment for their shareholders. If this required making creative use of hopelessly outdated and complex tax laws, or pressurising UK dairy farmers to provide milk at prices which pushed their operations to the brink of collapse, then so be it. Some went as far as claiming they were obliged to minimise their costs by any legal means available to them. Take for example Google's Matt Brittin, who appeared before the UK Parliament's Public Accounts Committee in November 2012 to answer for the alleged tax sins of his employers. In contrast to his two peers from Starbucks and Amazon—who meekly prostrate themselves in grovelling apologies and promised to change their ways—Mr Brittin was full of bravado. He explained that *of course*

Google minimises its tax bill by operating in Bermuda and Ireland—they were perfectly entitled to do so by international law. Google was simply fulfilling its duty to its shareholders to minimise its costs. Then there was the attitude of supermarkets such as Aldi, Asda, Morrisons and Lidl towards British dairy farmers. According to an article by David Gregory-Kumar for the BBC in August 2015, executives from these organisations argued that the struggles faced by their suppliers was not their problem. Their primary duty was to make a healthy return on investment while getting products to their customers at prices they were willing to pay.

Millennials are changing this way of thinking. Often referred to as Conscious Capitalists, their preference is to support businesses whose focus goes beyond profit, and instead serves the interest of their whole business ecosystem, creating and optimizing value for all of their stakeholders—customers, employees, investors, communities and suppliers alike. Organisations which operate in accordance with this philosophy are known as Conscious Businesses. These organisations are run by people who understand that strong and engaged stakeholders lead to a healthy, sustainable and resilient business. Their outlook is explained perfectly in the words of R. Edward Freeman, professor at the University of the Virginia Darden School of Business, and trustee of Conscious Capitalism, Inc.

> *We need red blood cells to live (the same way a business needs profits to live), but the purpose of life is more than to make red blood cells (the same way the purpose of business is more than simply to generate profits).*

Many conscious businesses actively demonstrate their commitment to Corporate Social Responsibility (CSR), and they publish their policies which serve as a guide to what the company represents for its consumers. CSR policies commonly focus on community involvement—sometimes local to where the business operates, while in other cases they may be involved in community projects which support fair trade practices for their suppliers. Environmental sustainability and ethical marketing are other common areas of focus. Having been born into a digital age Millennials are entirely at home with social media and use it to great effect—particularly when it comes to influencing the behaviour of organisations. Millennials want to know they are dealing with real human beings—not faceless organisations. They expect brands to interact and engage with them on social networks. Transparency and honesty are high up their list of essential characteristics of any organisation's CSR endeavours. This is what builds brand loyalty with Millennials, and they are quick to make good use of social media to punish organisations who fail to live up to their CSR promises.

Ultimately Millennials view corporations as more powerful than governments, and as a consequence they can use their economic vote as a means of influence far more effectively than their political vote.

17

Runescape and MMO Games

Sally has spent countless hours of her life playing Runescape. You may find it odd I chose the neutral word 'spent' rather than the prickly alternative 'wasted'. I also treated Runescape with the dignity of using its given name rather than referring more generally to 'stupid computer games'. I get it. 'Sally has wasted countless hours of her life playing stupid computer games' are the words I would have chosen but for the rather surprising reason that Sally credits Runescape with helping to reduce her anxiety and depression, as well as easing her off medication. For that Runescape deserves both respect and gratitude. I will try to explain what Runescape is in a single paragraph. But if I lose you along the way and you'd like a proper explanation, you may wish to turn to any of the thousands of online resources. You may even like to give it a try. It's free.

Runescape is a fantasy MMORPG which was originally released to a completely underwhelmed world in January 2001. At this point you may well be screaming *'STOP!!! What on earth is an MMORPG?'* For goodness sake, try to keep up. It's a Massively Multiplayer Online Role Playing Game. Think of it as comparable to Dungeons and Dragons, but on a computer and without the intimacy of sitting around a table with your mates sharing a pizza and a keg of beer. Got it? OK, let's continue. The game takes place in a medieval fantasy realm that players travel through on foot or using magical spells. Apparently it's even possible to charter ships, but I haven't got that far yet. The realm—which goes by the name of Gielinor—has its fair share of monsters to battle (or if you're a wuss like me; avoid). Players, who are represented in the game by avatars, set their own goals and objectives. There are quests to complete, and you can interact with other players through trading or chatting. You can also participate in an ever-expanding range of activities, some of which are competitive or combative in nature, while others require cooperation or collaboration.

The game was developed by the University of Cambridge graduate Andrew Gower, with help from his brothers Paul and Ian, and even artistic and audio input (in the form of the sound cooking bacon) from their primary school teacher mother, Gill. It has over 240 million accounts, which—I am proud to announce—now includes my account, *sallysmum*. Of the 240 million plus players, I suspect I am one of the oldest and most inept. Sadly I have endowed my avatar with my appalling real world sense of direction and spatial awareness. I am so focused on what my avatar is doing that I fail to notice the menacing goblins and monsters as they approach. As you would expect—given the hours of her life that she has dedicated to playing the game—Sally is awesome and knows the realm inside out. So enamoured is she that twice now, she has put aside her social anxiety to attended RuneFest, an annual event where aficionados of the game meet up in the real world for all manner of Runescape-related events. Sally is also my teacher—or rather she was until I fired her. The experience of having Sally as my Runescape tutor provided more than adequate evidence to confirm she is not cut out for the honourable profession of an educator; no teacher should roll around the floor in uncontrollable fits of laughter because of the inadequacies of their pupils. I'm sorry but that kind of behaviour clearly demonstrates an inappropriate level of commitment and tactfulness. Shame on you Sally.

Sally first came across Runescape when she was about 10 years old, having been introduced to it by her father during his stint as a house husband. While the girls were at school David filled his ample free time by indulging his passion for playing computer games. (He assures me he didn't just play games, but went shopping, tidied up, did the washing, even did a bit of DIY...but honestly, I don't remember seeing much evidence to back up this claim.) While Harriet had no interest in computer games (she whiled away her spare time lost in the world of Hogwarts with Harry Potter and his assortment of wizard and muggle friends), Sally seized whatever opportunity she could to get stuck into a feast of video games under the expert guidance of Daddy. In addition to Runescape, she also enjoyed playing The Sims—which is often described as a strategic, life-simulation game. Basically, players create a family of characters and have to take appropriate actions to keep their characters alive and well. Tasks such as hygiene, eating, getting a job and paying the bills are all essential, otherwise—like in the human world—their characters would suffer consequences for neglecting their own needs. So both Runescape and The Sims provided engaging ways for 10-year-old Sally to learn useful life skills, with the additional hope that they might trigger an interest in computer programming, or other such CV-enhancing activities.

David's games of choice involved intense virtual violence and blowing things up, rather than the nice child-friendly games he diligently researched before letting Sally loose on them. However unbeknown to me, Sally soon realised that the games played by her role-model father were far more entertaining than her own, and before long she started to develop a love of violent fantasy games such as PainKiller, BioShock and a whole host of others. I've been assured that these games weren't just about violence—they also involved strategic thinking and deeply philosophical decision making. For example in BioShock, players had to decide whether to harvest the powers of a helpless, innocent girl and run the risk of her exacting revenge at a later date, or let her keep her powers in the hope that she would become a useful ally in the future. I am pleased to report that my empath daughter never once harmed the girls—which is more than can be said for David.

Anyway, with this new and infinitely more exciting range of computer games to keep her busy, Sally forgot about the simple joys of Runescape until re-introduced to it about a decade later by a new boyfriend. Ten years is an exceptionally long time in the world of video games. Although the basic format remained the same, an immense amount of new content had been added in the form of greatly improved graphics, new characters, new quests, new lands and much, much more. And, as I mentioned earlier, the number of users had increased from the few thousand who played the early version, to a little short of a quarter of a billion. Along with a significant percentage of other players, Sally wasn't interested in the bright new shiny version. Instead, her loyalty lay with the simple pleasures of the decade-old version that she had enjoyed as a young child.

For a few glorious moments one Saturday, it appeared that her years of loyalty and dedication to Runescape had been rewarded. '*Muuuuuuummmmm, I can't believe I forgot to tell you my brilliant news*', she announced excitedly one afternoon after we'd spent the entire morning together chatting our way through a 5km sponsored walk next to Toilet Man and Turd Lady. (The walk was in aid of Crohn's and colitis UK, hence the rather unusual lavatorial costumes.) 'I've been invited to take part in BETA TESTING the new Runescape mobile application. I'm SOOOO happy. It's gonna be AMAZING!!!!' 'WOW Sally that sounds fantastic. You say you've known all morning? I don't understand how you could have *forgotten* to tell me something so important.' I replied with no more than a tiny hint of irony, before launching myself wholeheartedly onto her wave of enthusiasm. 'Where's it being held? What will you wear? Will there be a champagne reception? Can I come with you?' were just a few of the questions that spewed from my mouth, while visions of us being picked up by a black-suited chauffeur and whisked away Hollywood-style in a gold Limousine flashed wildly through my mind. Yeah. Right. I'm not stupid. Honestly, I'm not. I know from experience that Sally's 'amazing', 'unbelievable', 'mind-blowing' news won't be any of those things. I also know the wave of enthusiasm will rapidly disintegrate, leaving me face-down in the sand picking grit and fragments of shellfish from my teeth. This is one of life's certainties. And yet I willingly engage for a few seconds of adrenaline-fueled excitement, before the constraints of reality inevitably regain control, usually through a little nugget of information that I'd missed first time around. In this case the nugget was the fact that she'd been invited along with 9,999 others. Thankfully then, not much chance of a glitzy trip in a limo. I say *thankfully* because—even in my imagination—I was wearing my scruffy dog-walking jeans and a grey t-shirt emblazoned with the word *Vegan*, while being assisted into the magnificent carriage by an aloof chauffer who clearly thoroughly disapproved of my attire.

I suppose my reaction was similar to when an e-mail from NS&I Customer Service with the *title 'News from ERNIE about your NS&I Premium Bonds'* pops into my in-box. I've come to recognise this as notification I've won a prize in the National Savings and Investments monthly draw. I know the odds are stacked massively in favour of a £25 token gesture, rather than one of the two 1 million pound monthly windfalls. I know this, but for the few minutes it takes me to locate my personal ID and key it into their Prize Checker site, I fantasise about winning the top prize. For someone with such a vivid imagination, I am useless at imagining anything positive that would come out of a sudden influx of unearned money, and by the time I finally confirm my low-end prize, I'm actually quite relieved. (Or so I keep telling myself.)

There I go again. Off on one of my little detours. Let's get back to Sally's joy at being one of 10,000 invitees to beta test the new Runescape mobile application. It turns out that her excitement wasn't due to the invitation *per se*, but rather the fact that a mobile version was finally available after years of being forced to play from a laptop or static computer. Now she could play AFK—Away From Keyboard. Apparently this is a big deal. Personally I see it as just another safety hazard. I expect to come home one day to find her in a crumpled heap at the bottom of the stairs, frantically tapping away at her mobile phone and shouting '*die cave horrors, die*', as she's carefully lifted onto a stretcher and taken away to A&E.

If you cast your mind way back to the Prologue, you may recall me mentioning Sally's cunning plan to earn a bit of cash through live-streaming herself playing Runescape. 'So what's all this about?' I wonder out loud—as I'm sure you do too. Back to Google, 'why do people donate to streamers?' The first link, 30th August 2017, www.reddit.com perfectly reflected my own incredulity: *'So yeah, I am trying to understand the psychology behind people that tend to tip big ass streamers and I fail to understand it.'* As does the second, 7th Feb 2015, www.neogaf.com: *'I've been thinking about this for a bit now, and for some reason I can't wrap my head around why someone would throw 100's and 1000's to streamers?'* And the third—my favourite—30 Dec 2017, www.mmo-champion.com *'Literally what the fuck? What* do people even get out of donating this much amount of money to a random dude on the internet?'

Clearly many people have asked this question before. Like me, I'm sure you want answers. So here are three of the top reasons adapted from the first link.

1 Entertainment value: people pay to watch all sorts of thing—football, opera, Netflix. Why not great gameplay, funny content, great banter and the like? Ummm, seems to be a bit of a flaw in this argument—something about voluntary donations vs purchase, but let's not get too picky.
2 Attention: Ego and/or narcissism. Some donations come from those who just like to see their own name and donation amount pop up on the screen.
3 Boobs: Apparently '*White knights*[10] *will donate to hot gamer*

10 Urban Dictionary definition of White Knight (corrected to replace the grammatical disaster of *'a womens right'... Sorry, but these things matter*): A man who stands up for a woman's right to be an absolute equal, but then steps up like a *white knight* to rescue her any time that equality becomes a burden.

gurrl streamers against all logic.' The post goes on to caution *'If you're a dude, this probably won't work out too well for you.'*

In the immortal words of Bristol's favourite son, comedian Russell Howard—I SHIT YOU NOT. With no financial outlay other than a half-decent webcam, Sally could make pots of money simply by flashing a bit of cleavage, while playing a game she loves and is awesome at. I don't remember seeing that on her school's list of career options!

I'm sure you can guess the next subject I want to explore—just how much money could she make? Thanks to a YouTube video[11] from Joe Osrs, I can tell you that back in July 2016 the top 3 streamers averaged in excess of £40,000 each from donations alone. The chances are they also made plenty more from subscriptions, advertisements and product sales. Earning serious money from doing something you enjoy—that's got to be living the dream.

So now I'd become enthusiastic about Sally's possible choice of career, she suddenly went off the idea. Kids hey, it's impossible to fathom them out. Just when you think you've made a breakthrough in understanding their world, they change their mind and you're right back to square one. Sally claimed it was something to do with being concerned about making a fool of herself in front of a camera, and the footage being forever available to come back and haunt her. Personally I have no such worries for myself, and I have added live streaming Runescape to my retirement plan. Expect to see my account *sallysmum* active on Twitch or other streaming service sometime soon. Maybe I'll even reinstate Sally as my tutor, and we can stream her teaching me how to play. Now that would be entertainment that even I would donate to watch.

11 https://www.youtube.com/watch?v=iPR8uq1qnzo

18

Virtual Reality

Thanks to Virtual Reality I now know for certain what it feels like to experience a totally irrational fear. One day at work I was busy at my desk when I heard the occasional short yelp from the far corner of the office. It came from an area where strange goings-on with VR headsets were not uncommon, but I had never bothered to investigate. It took similar expressions of fear from four or five different people before my curiosity got the better of me, and I wandered the 30 metres or so towards the source of the activity to find out what was going on. Well, what was going on BLEW MY MIND. I was offered a headset which instantly transported me into the heart of London. I landed in the Westminster area of the virtual city. My view of the surroundings was similar to what Roald Dahl's Big Friendly Giant would experience if he were to visit the city today. The clock face of Big Ben was just below my head height. Nearby on the other side of the River Thames, the London Eye loomed large in my field of vision. As I looked around awestruck, a voice from the real world asked me if I'd like to take the 'Plank Challenge'. Obviously, I accepted. It would have been rude to decline the kind invitation. The challenge involved getting into a virtual lift, pressing a virtual button and being transported to the 100th floor of a virtual building. Easy Peasy. On arrival, the virtual doors of the virtual lift opened directly into the virtual outside world. Glancing down, I saw a virtual plank extending into what felt like an exceedingly real and terrifying void. A voice from back in the safety of the office suggested that I stepped out onto the plank. Very, very nervously I did as I was asked, and put one foot in front of the other. I stood there for a few seconds not daring to look down, before the disembodied voice returned and said 'now step off the end of the plank', at which point an exceedingly real fear took over. My rational brain was fully engaged telling me I had nothing to worry about—I knew exactly where I was in the real world, and I was 100% certain there were no real world hazards to be concerned about. I knew my fear was completely irrational, and yet it held me utterly in its grip. My feet were rooted to the spot, and I was totally unable to undertake the simple task of taking a small step on a perfectly safe office floor. I pulled off the headset and was returned to the safety of the office with a dramatically increased heart rate, a feeling of shameful failure, and a real understanding of how powerful and all-consuming irrational fears can be.

Regressing to the state of an excited child at Christmas, I exchanged a flurry of texts with Sally in which both sides of the conversation included words such as *AMAZING!!!!, UNBELIEVABLE!!!* And, from Sally, *Whaaaaaaaaaat!!!! I'm so jealous...* I also returned to the real world convinced that the imaginary adventure playground of my childhood daydreams was getting ever closer to becoming a reality.

Although the rapid advancement of VR is being driven by the high-end gaming industry, its usefulness is being explored in many other domains. One area where I feel certain it has an exciting future is in transforming the tourism industry. My desire to explore and experience exciting new locations was a significant reason behind the creation of my imaginary childhood world. But while I still love the *idea* of visiting historic buildings, landscapes, cultures and civilisations, the *reality* is often impossible, prohibitively expensive or ends up proving to be a massive disappointment.

Take, for example, a recent visit to the Vatican, where Saint Peter's Basilica and the Sistine Chapel were high on my list of places to see. Although I have no real interested in either art or religion, I do have a love of the Renaissance architecture of Rome and the Vatican, as well as a deep respect for the technical brilliance of Michelangelo. I purchased the tickets in advance so we could avoid queueing, and made sure we arrived before 9am, our allocated time of entry. I knew we wouldn't be able to avoid the crowds—after all, our trip coincided with the height of the holiday season—but I wasn't prepared for the hour or more of misery I had to endure prior to arriving at my ultimate destination. My expectation was we would spend a short time strolling through a few cavernous rooms and airy corridors, where I could admire priceless historic artefacts at my leisure. Then, in a perfectly relaxed state, enter into the serene, awe-inspiring Sistine Chapel where I would spend half an hour or so in quiet contemplation of the amazing achievement of Leonardo, his team of artists and of humanity in general. With the benefit of hindsight, I now realise that this expectation contained all the ingredients of my own personal brand of blind optimism, mixed in with an unhealthy—and inexplicable—dose of naivety. If I'd envisioned a visit which bore even a passing resemblance to the reality, I would have planned my day in the Vatican very differently. It started well enough; we did indeed waltz our way past the massed ranks of tourists who queued patiently in a line that stretched from the entrance all the way to infinity. After a quick security check we passed through the turnstiles where we joined a million or so other early starters who had presumably beamed in from another planet. I can find no other sensible explanation for how so many people had been processed through the entrance and a limited number of security guards in the 15 minutes that had elapsed since the published 9am opening time. From there we passed into a number of rooms and corridors which—as I had predicted—were filled to the brim with paintings, sculptures, tapestries, models and all manner of other priceless historic artefacts. For a time, while my levels of energy and enthusiasm where still at their peak, I recall enjoying the experience. But before long things started to go downhill, as a growing mass of sweaty, noisy humans was corralled through endless and increasingly suffocating corridors. As we progressed at a painfully slow pace towards the ultimate goal, the ever-increasing temperature and constant bombardment of my senses drained my energy. I soon reached the point where I'd lost interest in the surroundings and switched my entire focus to reaching the exit without having to call on emergency services to resuscitate me. By the time I entered the Sistine Chapel, I was exhausted. My elation did not result from admiration for the work of Michelangelo, but from the utter relief of knowing the ordeal was coming to an end, and I would soon be outside recovering in the sunshine while enjoying a cold, refreshing drink.

This had not been the relaxed, enjoyable experience I had hoped for, but rather had many features associated with my most disturbing (but mercifully rare) nightmares. The visit was so unpleasant that I'm unlikely to attempt it—or indeed anything similar—ever again. But that doesn't mean I won't one day be able to enjoy a leisurely stroll through a highly realistic virtual equivalent—without the crowds and exhausting pre-arrival ordeal. The Sistine Chapel has already been imaged in high definition, and is available as a virtual tour. I'm convinced that in just a few years from now, technology will improve to the point where it will be possible to explore the Vatican—and indeed many sites of interest—in a fully immersive, virtual world. A world in which sights, sounds, smells and touch combine with high-speed internet connectivity to other pre-selected travellers and tour guides. That's when travel will become fun and relaxing again, and that's when I'll start my World Tour.

A trip to Machu Picchu in Peru is high up my list of dream destinations. But I don't want the hassle and expense of a long, arduous flight and death-defying coach trip. Neither do I want to drag my aging body through the ruins of the ancient site in the heat of the day accompanied by an army of tourists. No, I would rather my experience occurred in the era when the location was at its peak condition and home to a thriving pre-Columbian community. I would also like the visit to take place from the comfort and convenience of my own home whenever I have a few hours to spare. OK, so I know this wish list goes a long way beyond the world's current technical capabilities, but in ten years from now I fully expect this scenario to be possible.

By the time I reach my 70s, my Saturday morning activities could involve mundane tasks such as getting up, having breakfast, taking the dog for a walk then pulling on my sensory suit, switching on my VR kit and selecting my chosen destination. Let's say I'm off to Isabela Island in the Galapagos, where I have arranged to meet up with family and friends for an afternoon exploring the island in search of the giant tortoises that roam freely across the unspoilt landscape. This leisurely trek leads us to a perfect location for a relaxing picnic. Here we sit and eat lunch (real food and drink, prepared before entering the virtual world) while engaging in conversation and indulging in a spot of whale and dolphin watching. Fully refreshed, our journey continues towards an entrancing golden beach. Carefully avoiding the Sally Lightfoot crabs on our short walk across the pristine sand, we make our way to the warm, shallow waters of the Pacific for a refreshing paddle with the resident Galapagos penguins. A perfect day in one of the most precious environments on Earth, surrounded by family, friends and a selection of local tour guides, at a fraction of the price of the real thing. No long-distance flights, no damage to the fragile island ecosystem, no expensive health insurance for the over 60s, no access limitations for disabled or infirm visitors. All of these benefits and back in time to give the dog his dinner. Perfect. Maybe later in the day I could squeeze in a quick visit to Transylvania to catch up with my maternal ancestors, followed by a scuba diving trip in Tasmania to experience play time with a family of duck-billed platypus.

Other areas where Virtual Reality has a massively exciting future is as therapy for a wide range of mental health disorders, desensitisation to phobias and even as an aid to stop smoking. There is growing confidence among the clinical community that VR simulations will become a common tool in their arsenal, working alongside medication and traditional talking therapies. In the US for example, the University of Sothern California has been running the *Bravemind: VR Exposure Therapy Project* for well over a decade to treat post-traumatic stress disorder in servicemen returning from warzones. Therapy involves placing the patient in a virtual warzone in which a clinician can create realistic simulations tailored to the experience of each individual. In addition to the visual stimuli presented in the VR head-mounted display, audio, vibrations and smells can be delivered into the simulation. Prior to VR, therapy relied heavily on PTSD sufferers imagining a particular scenario. But this approach is often severely restricted by the ability or willingness of the patient to recreate a mental image of the real-world events that are at the heart of their debilitating condition. With VR, patients can be immersed in a highly realistic virtual recreation of the circumstances that have been haunting their mind. Simulations that have the power to create strong emotional responses, but under safe and controlled conditions. Bravemind is now a well-established programme, with equipment and trained therapists available at over 100 military bases in the US, and expanding elsewhere.

Compared to the US, therapeutic use of VR in the UK is still in its infancy but seems certain to grow. In 2017, as part of their Make it Digital series, BBC3 explored the work of Michael Carthy—a therapist with clinics in London and Dublin—who uses VR simulations alongside traditional therapies to accelerate the treatment of phobias. The documentary showed how his therapy helped a young woman deal with an anxiety disorder related to her fear of being trapped in an enclosed space. After just a few short sessions in which she was exposed to virtual representations of lifts and the London Underground, she was able to overcome her deep-rooted fear and handle situations which had for so long been impossible for her.

19

Insomnia

Before Harriet came along, I had no problem getting a good night's sleep. A full 8 hours was normal, and this could easily stretch to 9 or even 10 at weekends when I wasn't roused from my slumber by a pesky alarm clock. As a new mother I expected sleepless nights, and that's exactly what I got. However, when my squealing first-born eventually settled into a regular pattern of undisturbed, blissful night time slumber, I expected to do the same. Sadly it seems the Sandman's resources didn't extend to triple occupancy of our home. So while Harriet and David enjoyed a full quota of his nightly sprinkling of sand, I was consistently short-changed. All he had left to offer was enough to get me off to sleep, but insufficient to sustain me for over 4 hours.

In 25 years since Harriet was born, I have never once managed a full night's undisturbed sleep. Not once. By the end of this year that will equate to over 9,500 continuous nights! Usually I'll wake up around 2am and then struggle to navigate my way back to the Land of Nod. Although I eventually find my way back and sneak in unnoticed through an unguarded entrance, it's usually only 40 minutes before the well-trained and vigilant bouncers track me down and eject me, forcing me to go through the entire process again.

Over the years I have tried many methods to beat this problem. Some—such as giving up vast quantities of caffeine after lunch time—have definitely helped, but nothing I've tried has ever restored me to my pre-motherhood state. And believe me, I've tried plenty of different approaches; I've counted more sheep than have ever existed in Australia and New Zealand combined; I've experimented with all sorts of breathing exercises; I've tried toe-scrunching and other exercise-based approaches; I've listened to soothing music, white noise and relaxation videos—sometimes all at the same time. No matter what I've tried, natural approaches just don't get me more than a 40 minute extension before I'm awake again. Even unnatural approaches in the shape of tiny, bullet-shaped capsules are only marginally more effective.

From time to time my inability to sleep has been a blessing. For example, the time I was staying in a hotel in the depths of the Surrey countryside when I was fortunate enough to witness the dawn chorus. It was the most beautiful, uplifting, life-enhancing sound I had ever heard. It was so entrancing that I got out of bed, threw on some clothes, and removed myself from the confines of my hotel bedroom. I navigated my way out into the gardens and past a startled dark red fox, before heading towards an area of mature trees. Once there, I lay down on the grass and enjoyed the spectacular avian performance while breathing in the cool, fragranced early morning air. It was heaven. It didn't concern me in the slightest that it was 4 o'clock in the morning, the grass was moist with dew or that I'd forgotten to put on any footwear. Although I had less than 5 hours sleep that night, I was relaxed and had no problem concentrating throughout the demanding day that followed. This led me to think 5 hours may be enough, as long as I spend another few hours during the night in a relaxed state, rather than fretting about how I'll get through the following day as an exhausted wreck.

Since that blissful morning, I have often lay awake wishing I could recreate the experience, or an equally inspiring alternative. Maybe I could transport myself to the heart of a forest where I could look up and see a beautiful starry night sky and hear the distant sounds of an assortment of nocturnal creatures; or watch the sunrise while listening to rustling leaves accompanied by a light and cooling breeze. Sadly, the rich visual imagery I conjured up with ease during my childhood has faded. Instead I'm unable to escape from my real-world surroundings which all too often includes a messy bedroom and the disturbing sound of my husband snoring.

Occasionally I scout around the Internet in the hope of discovering a product to relieve the nightly tedium of my insomnia. Something that could conjure up the vibrant, realistic scenes my faded visual imagery can no longer muster. Virtual Reality would be perfect—but without the need to wear a cumbersome headset and ear phones. So far I've not found anything that comes close. A tiny voice in my head pops up from time to time with a somewhat surprising suggestion. 'Stop waiting for someone else to create a solution', it whispers, 'do it yourself.' While another dismissive—and much louder—voice replies, 'don't be stupid, you're an IT consultant, you wouldn't have a clue!' But recently—in fact since I started writing this book and exploring a new world of opportunities—the first voice has been getting louder and more persistent, while the second is showing signs of giving up in a teenage strop with retorts along the lines of 'Yeh, whatever...go make a fool of yourself if that's what you want.'

The dialogues going on inside my head bear an uncanny resemblance (in nature, if not content) to the underlying theme of Phineas and Ferb—one the cartoons I regularly enjoyed while Sally was growing up. (Yes. *Enjoyed.* Don't judge me—there's a lot of great stuff on Disney Channel!) Basically, step-brothers Phineas and Ferb are always coming up with new and exciting projects to fill the 104 days of their summer vacation. Big sister Candice never approves and spends her days trying to stop them by telling tales. For example in Rollercoaster—the first ever episode—Phineas and Ferb are busy constructing a massive rollercoaster in their back garden (sorry, back yard, they live in America), Candice goes off in search of Mom to tattle on them. Of course Mom doesn't believe Candice, and by the time she gets back home all evidence of the rollercoaster had disappeared. (It would probably be too much of an unnecessary distraction to explain how this happened—all I will say is it involved Perry, their pet platypus. I find it strange how the platypus has wormed its way into this book on so many levels.)

Anyway, back to the dialogue in my head. One day, while the annoyingly negative resident of my mind—which I'll call Candice—was otherwise engaged, I gave its inventive, but easily ignored cranial room-mate Phineas (Ferb doesn't speak, he's the master craftsman of the pair) a chance to present its thoughts. And what Phineas told me was enlightening. Firstly, it explained that I had (or could call upon members of my family to provide), the majority of the skills needed to build a simple prototype. My engineering background would be invaluable in the structural design of the 'pod', while Harriet's Diploma in Interior Design would surely help ensure it is pleasing on the eye. As would her woodworking skills which, under the ever-patient guidance of David, have rapidly advanced. Sally's sewing skills could be used for creating the outer skin, while her increasing mastery of photography and Photoshop could be called on for creating the images. Her sound-engineer boyfriend could provide the soundtracks, or we could simply purchase them from an existing database. Both of my social media savvy daughters could be relied on to find the most thoroughly modern ways to market the product.

'Yeh, but you've got no chance of making it anywhere close to realistic', chips in Candice, who had sneaked back in unnoticed. 'You're absolutely right', confirms Phineas, 'it won't be anywhere close to realistic'. But then, instead of running into the safety of a dark corner to hide, Phineas stood its ground and added 'But that doesn't matter. It can still be useful without being perfect.' 'How so?' retorts Candice in its usual mocking tone. Phineas went on to explain how there were many uses for the idea which could be built on over time as technology improved.

Firstly, a basic model which fitted around a bed could provide a blackout environment for night-shift workers who found themselves having to get off to sleep in the early afternoon during the height of summer. We could easily add calming sounds of nature—for example waves crashing against the shore or a distant thunderstorm—to help distract from normal urban sounds of conversations, traffic and the occasional pneumatic drill. Or we could investigate more expensive options such as noise-cancelling speakers, or sound absorbing fabrics. It wouldn't even matter if high quality visual imagery isn't feasible at a reasonable cost, after all this is supposed to be a relaxing environment, not a full-on cinematic experience. Instead, it shouldn't be too difficult to project the colours of sunset and sunrise, while synchronising their timings to the requirements of each individual user. We could also include a small fan to provide a cooling breeze and disperse a relaxing fragrance of essential oils. With a little electronic wizardry, fragrances could be released just in time to welcome the sleeper gently back into a glorious new sunny day. Then, refreshed, relaxed and eager to embark on a new day, they leave the protective cocoon and re-enter the real world. Back there, it is ten o'clock on a typical British summer's evening (i.e. pouring with rain) and the sun has set for the night. Sorry, but I have no plans for fixing that particular problem.

At this point, I feel it is my duty to perform a public service and draw your attention to a shocking revelation that was recently reported in the Science section of the Telegraph. Scientific studies have shown that lavender, tea tree and other essential oils can cause an array of health problems, including triggering the development of man-boobs in pre-pubescent boys. Catching a whiff of another 'fake news' story designed to destabilise the western economy by causing a global crash in the price of lavender and tea tree oil, I dug further to discover the report did indeed appear to be accessible through the genuine Telegraph website. Choose your fragrances carefully—you have been warned!

Back to the conversation that was playing out in my head. Phineas went on to describe the possibilities of a relaxation pod which fitted around your favourite arm chair rather than your bed. This would allow people to transport themselves into a world of their choice while they engaged in relaxing activities such as reading a book or listening to their favourite radio show. For example the user could instantly be transported to the deck of a boat that is floating on a calm lake surrounded by snow-topped mountains, the sound of waves gently lapping against the hull, while in the distance a range of waterfowl tend to their young.

Convinced that Phineas was on to something, I floated the concept to Sally—my go-to person for crazy ideas—who was, as usual, very supportive. Or at least she was until I included my thoughts on important practicalities which included getting a business loan from a bank. 'Really Mother, you're so out of touch. That is *not* how you do things these days', she said in her most serious and professional tone, while placing a strong emphasis on the word 'not'. 'It's about time you learned about crowdfunding', she continued. 'Let me show you how Kickstarter works.' And so yet another enthralling journey into the magical modern world began. I had previously come across the concept of crowdfunding as a means of quickly raising money for urgent health treatment. For instance, I knew the concept had been used to repatriate a seriously injured local teenager after he'd been in a quad bike accident that was not covered by his travel insurance. But until this point I had not realised it was a serious option for raising money for a business idea.

Kickstarter is an American public-benefit corporation—a form of non-profit organisation—whose primary focus is on supporting creative projects. It is one of a growing number of crowdfunding platforms, but unlike many of the others—or indeed the more traditional approaches for raising investment capital—it claims no ownership over the projects or the work they create. Personally I find the success of the concept mind-blowing. It works by creators pitching their ideas along with a solid plan, a funding goal, a deadline for raising the funds and a set of tangible rewards or experiences in return for pledges. Backers pledge funds to those projects which interest them by selecting their chosen reward. If the funding target is met by the deadline, the creator is guaranteed to receive the pledges and Kickstarter takes a small percentage cut. The only future responsibility of the creator is to provide the promised rewards to the backers. If the funding target isn't met, no money is exchanged, and the project is closed down.

My highly unlikely entrepreneurial journey will get underway just as soon as this book has been safely delivered into the world. As of now, I have no idea how I'll overcome the challenges which stand between me and my vision for 'the pod'. Absolutely clueless. Firstly there's the problem of naming it. Sally switched on her creative brain to produce a logo for Zen Den. Unfortunately, after a quick search on the Intellectual Property Office website, I realised the name was already taken. As was my second choice, Urban Zen. Not a great start—and this is the easy part. I'm sure the technical difficulties we'll face will be daunting, but I won't let that put me off. What was it I said before? I AM NOT A QUITTER. The project will take me on a journey of discovery. I've no idea how long it will take but there's no rush[12] and I'm planning on having a heap of fun on the way. Of course, there may already be a product out there that I haven't come across yet. If you're aware of something, please let me know. I'd like a fall-back plan just in case Phineas and Ferb have over-estimated their capability on this occasion.

12 This is not strictly true. My mother and my aunty Doreen, who are both in their 80s want one so they can enjoy the freedom of the great outdoors from the comfort of their living rooms. In the case of Mum, it would also greatly reduce the risk of her tripping over the kerb, knocking out another 2 teeth and having to go to A&E for a couple of stitches in her face again. What a drama queen! Sorry gals, but you might have to hang on in there for a few more years.

20

Retirement Planning

So far the focus of this story has been on the past and present. Now I'd like to end with a quick peek forward at my hopes for how the future will unfold.

I have to admit that way back when I was writing the Prologue, and first used *three-quarter life crisis*, I thought I'd invented the term. The prospect of nurturing a brand new expression through infancy all the way to becoming an established member of the English language filled me with a strange sense of awe and responsibility. Not on the same level as my first pregnancy of course, nevertheless it was exciting. I don't normally bother with New Year's resolutions, but 2018 started with the commitment to get my very own expression into common use. Sadly my excitement lasted only as long as it took me to Google the phrase. It's been used before. Not a huge amount, and there's no formally accepted definition, but it's already out there. The Urban Dictionary defines it as the *depression, ennui, and disorientation experienced when, for the first time in your life, you lose your job AND you are over the age of 55*. Yes, I can see how that sucks and could lead to a personal crisis. For my part I feel this definition is too restrictive, and it certainly doesn't match my own situation. Neither does it fit with the experience of Michael Cosgrove, whose own three-quarter life crisis at the age of 60 had nothing to do with losing his job. His crisis—which led him to embark on a long and dangerous attempt to sail around the world—was triggered by wanting to leave a legacy for his family, combined with his despair at the prospect of growing old. I think he succeeded with his voyage—he certainly made it back to shore to write a book: Imperfect Passage.

So, several months ago I discovered that *three-quarter life crisis* was already active in the English language. It was no big deal. I could still use the term. It's not like there was a copyright on it, or even a universally agreed definition. Though, as I immersed myself in writing *Mother of Millennials*, it gradually dawned on me that the expression wasn't appropriate for my own circumstances. Firstly I am *definitely not* in the midst of a crisis. I have no plans to chuck in my job and put my life at risk sailing around the world. No thank you. My situation is not nearly that disruptive or desperate. I'm doing nothing more demanding than taking a calm, measured look into the future. What I see there is a whole host of interesting and exciting possibilities to fuel me through the remainder of my time on this earth, without subjecting myself to a single personal hardship. In my case '*awakening*' seems to be far more appropriate than '*crisis*'. Then there's the numbers. By the time this book is published I'll be 57, which is ¾ of 76. Sorry, but I'm planning on being a living, breathing human for much more than another 19 years. Reassuringly the life expectancy calculator available through the BBC website backs me up. According to this, a 57-year-old female from England has an average life expectancy of 87. That's more like it. Another 30 years, or just short of ELEVEN THOUSAND days. Hell, if I put my mind to it I'm sure I can pack a lot of craziness into 11,000 days. One more calculation and I promise the maths is over. 57 (my current age) divided by 87 (my average life expectancy) is—as near as damn it—two thirds. So there you have it. Rather than going through *a three-quarter life crisis*, I'm actually experiencing a *two-third life awakening*. I have just Googled the term, and I can confirm that there are NO HITS. Nothing even comes close. I hereby claim it as my own invention and assign the following definition:

> Two-third life awakening: the period in your life when you realise your children will be a drain on your finances for much

longer than expected. But instead of getting stressed, you decide to make life-enhancing plans to ensure the Bank of Mum and Dad remains open for business.

To qualify for inclusion, the life-enhancing plans must make you happy AND be capable of earning money. It doesn't have to be much, just enough to keep Bank of Mum and Dad ticking over. As I was writing the last sentence I was hit by the realisation that the part before the comma is unlikely to achieve the part after it. But let's be optimistic and go with it anyway. In fact, I think I'll make optimism part of the deal for having a two-third life awakening. As the inventor of the term, I'm well within my rights to make whatever rules I want. Besides, if you lack a sunny, positive nature, you may find the more established three-quarter life crisis better suited to your needs.

Seriously though, if you are a stranger to optimism, you should give it a try. I can't imagine how I would have got through Sally's mental illness if I'd not been able to call on an endless supply of positivity. I'm sure it would have been pure hell for both of us—and made Sally's progress along the path to recovery so much more difficult—if my natural reaction had been to fear the worst, obsess over what could go wrong and blame life for being such a complete and utter bitch. If optimism doesn't come naturally to you, it's never too late to learn. Indeed this could be the first new skill on your to-do list. If you don't know where to start, just Google *learn to be an optimist* and let the road trip begin.

Here's another reason to give two-third life awakening a try: if it turns out you suck at it, you've not missed out. There's still time to embark on a full-blown three-quarter life crisis in the knowledge that you thoroughly deserve it. So you've got nothing to lose, really.

Once you decide to commit to a two-third life awakening you could get started by dusting off under-utilised or long-forgotten skills. Then put them to work through online shops, video channels, or other Internet-enabled magic that your children's generation has been quietly implementing while you've been consumed by your busy, stressful life. Alternatively, dig out all those boxes of disturbing art work you created as a stressed-out, overwhelmed new parent, and sell it all on eBay or Etsy or any other of the multitude of online shops. Then create some more that represent your current state of mind and repeat the selling process.

There's also the potential to earn serious money from the Internet in the guise of entertainment, for instance by uploading videos. Of course, the videos have to be engaging enough to get many thousands of people positively excited by them, and willing to subscribe, donate, purchase related products, or demonstrate support using a multitude of other money-generation techniques.

The greatest success is often achieved with minimal effort, especially if you have easy access to a cute dog with a particularly unusual ability, disability or —ideally—both. Loca, the Singing Pug, is an example of this phenomenon. This talented pooch (sadly now deceased) had both a mild neurological condition and an amazing ability as a singer-songwriter. Hailing from Belfast, Loca enjoyed a stellar rise to internet stardom by using her talents to show how perfect her life was—despite the fact that she couldn't run. Chances are that once you've watched it, you'll find it impossible to stop singing the joyous refrain '*Dancing, prancing, falling all around the show*', while rhythmically pressing the 'Donate Now' button.

Want to know how to earn money from a talented pet?
Check out Loca the Singing Pug.

I won't claim any of this will be easy, it's not supposed to be. It's about challenging yourself outside the realm of your day job. It's also about preparing an enjoyable little side-line to top up your vulnerable pension when—as seems increasingly likely—a Millennial-controlled government launches a raid on your funds. If you've survived long enough to have grown-up children, you're certain to have amassed an extensive array of useful skills you take for granted. Work out what these skills are and embark on a journey to use them. Alternatively, you might want to try learning new ones. Like me, you could decide to write a book, learn how to use Social Media as a marketing tool, create a relaxation pod, learn to program applications for mobile phones, live-stream yourself playing Runescape, experience the joys of using a kick-ass electric saw that could take your arm off in a single moment of carelessness, or any number of other crazy schemes that will no doubt pop into my now finely tuned entrepreneurial brain. It might not be easy, but do you think Boyan Slat's little project to remove billons of empty crisp packets and bottles of tomato ketchup from the great expanse of the world's oceans is easy? Hell no! But he's not letting that stop him—and he's still a mere youngster. Just think what you can do with the twin benefits of age and experience to call on.

Now that I've invented *two-third life awakening*, formally claimed the right to be recognised as its inventor, defined the term and explained exactly what it means, I've got about 11,000 days (assuming all goes well) to get the term officially recognised in the English language before I kick the bucket. I know that sounds like a long time—and happily it is. But there's no time like the present. If you don't mind, I'd like to get started by asking all you 50 somethings out there to help me out on this. *Two-third life awakening* is not copyrighted. Google it, Tweet it, Blog it, #TWOTHIRDLIFEAWAKENING it. But most of all, Live It.

If you started at the Prologue and have got this far, thank you. I am truly grateful. But don't leave me now (you'll take away the biggest part of me...) Why not join me and my amazing daughters at MotherofMillennials.co.uk. Whatever your age, you'll be very welcome to join us with what I hope will be entertaining and enlightening inter-generational bonding.

Lightning Source UK Ltd.
Milton Keynes UK
UKHW01f1113130918
328818UK00002B/67/P